# KRISHNA MOHAN AVANCHA

# The Art Needed for WINNING Job WAR!!!

# Contents

# 1

# Introduction

I am no saint or a person born with a golden spoon but for 2 straight years I too have struggled to find my feet back in the job market. I too have been rejected countless times, insulted by many and told I was not the right candidate but something which helped me pull my weight back on and start was a simple but effective desire to be someplace better. I kept going because of my wish to write so that at least one person could read my book and get benefited from it. I still write with this only expectation. Hoping someday at least one person will walk up to me and thank me for the help my book gave him or at least meet me at random with my book in their hand hoping to discuss with me on the same.

I know this is far long but it is always good to have something that you can fight for a dream you would like to die for. Also it will help you get by life when it throws you a curve ball or a bouncer.

It is during these tough times that these dreams will help to stand up and smile at them as you keep looking at the sunrise at the end of this period. Let's all of us stand up and strive for the dream to be able to provide for our families all that they ask and want as that is one of all of our prime instincts and reasons for the fight.

A very good quote comes to my mind at this point which I had heard in a movie,"Once more into the fray, Into the **last good fight I'll ever know**. Live and die on this day. Live and die on this day", movie Gray.

The reason for this recital is,"**everyone has to die at some point, but it is what kind of a life someone lived that will determine their outcome**."

Hope you too find solace in this recital as I do even to this day. Do write back to me if you feel I could in any way support your getting up as would like to be part of your success story if possible. I might not be able to write quickly to everyone but believe when I say it that if there is any possibility that I could help in re writing your resume or helping you get through an interview or just helping you with a few good words in whatever time I am left with I will be happy to use it for each one of you as I know this pain and have dealt with it for a long period of time.

Here's me wishing you all the best in your endeavors and hoping you can write back if you get benefited by me on krishnamrrao@gmail.com.

# 2

# Which skills do you need the most and how to learn them?

These are the 22 most in-call for abilities universal, in keeping with the reports from linkedin, upwork and adobe:

blockchain development.
   Many organizations are seeking to put in force blockchain era of their everyday operations. If you understand the ins and outs of blockchain generation and decentralized networks, your know-how can be attractive to employers. Cloud and disbursed computing. Employers seek personnel who can supply and manipulate assets through the net and a conversation network. Enjoy with cloud web hosting offerings can earn you a niche on employers' want lists.

Search engine optimization.
   With search engine optimization experience, you'll apprehend how serps prioritize seek outcomes based totally on factors together with links and key phrases. Corporations place high importance on search engine optimization talents,

as they're key to growing website traffic.

Virtual truth (vr) development.

Vr and augmented reality packages facilitate simulated stories that mimic the actual world. As many organizations are looking for to amplify their digital presence, the range of positions for vr builders has extended. Facts evaluation. The potential to paintings with data of a wide variety is imperative for a big range of employers.

Cell development.

Understanding how to create and expand apps for diverse styles of devices is taken into consideration a plus, given the big use of apps.

Scientific computing.

Additionally known as computational science, medical computing refers back to the equipment and theories needed to solve complicated math issues using computers. With demand for pc science jobs increasing, having this talent let you stand out to employers.

Analytical reasoning.

The ability to evaluate data and make logical judgments may be specially precious to employers which have open positions for business analysts and accountants.

Artificial intelligence.

With all the growth throughout technology fields, businesses need devices and structures which could increase on human intelligence and perform complicated duties.

Web structure and development.

In case you are professional in operating with software frameworks that assist to simplify the development of web applications, you will be enormously trendy through many employers.

Algorithm layout.

In case you are professional at developing simple steps to remedy complicated issues, there are lots of employers so that it will want to paintings with you.

Commercial enterprise evaluation.

Commercial enterprise proprietors are continuously looking to develop their groups. With commercial enterprise evaluation skills, you could assist businesses discover areas for alternate and make the proper adjustments.

Java improvement.

In case you are an expert at the usage of this famous programming language, you will be incredibly useful to an array of agencies and corporations. Affiliate advertising. Via associate advertising, a corporation can pay a 3rd birthday party for selling its merchandise. Associate marketing capabilities can make you more appealing to organizations that need to get their brands in the front of a larger target audience.

Machine gaining knowledge of.

With information of system mastering, you'll have an expertise of a way to broaden pc systems that use statistics and algorithms to improve over time. All kinds of employers are searching out employees with this skill. Consumer enjoy (ux) layout. In case you are skilled in ux layout, you'll know how to create merchandise that are clean and exciting for customers to use and, in flip, help companies collect and keep customers. C++ programming. For the reason that c++ is taken into consideration one of the oldest and maximum green programming languages, being skilled in it is considered a major asset by way of groups of all kinds. Mysql programming. Because mysql is the outstanding language for including, accessing and handling content in a database, folks that are skilled in the use of this language are needed inside the staff.

Project control:

with experience or a certification in venture control, you may be capable of oversee and cope with projects of all kinds, as a consequence making you plenty greater valuable inside the place of business.

Video manufacturing and editing.

In case you own video modifying and filming skills, there are lots of employers so that it will rent you to produce content for advertising functions. Income. The capability to hook up with clients and promote products or services will constantly make you a relatively attractive candidate to various styles of employers.

Enterprise development.

In case you understand the way to help companies grow, construct partnerships and attain new heights, many small and midsize groups should use your assist. A way to collect in-call for abilties

in case you lack in-demand capabilities, there are several

methods you may get revel in in those regions and boom your appeal to employers. Even though one of the maximum common ways to study new capabilities is to wait college and get a degree, there are some different processes you may take to expand your talent set.

1. Take a web path. You may work via on line guides at your personal tempo, and there are numerous cheaper or loose alternatives. For example, udemy offers instructions beginning at $14. Ninety nine. Stanford has many unfastened guides in regions consisting of gadget studying, database layout and cryptography (a blockchain essential). If you opt to soar thru content material freely, you could discover in-depth youtube films from specialists on pretty much any ability imaginable.

2. Research at your contemporary process. You may not be capable of research certain skills for your normal role at work, but there's bound to be someone on your place of work who has one or a number of the talents you want to acquire. Attain out to colleagues in other departments or a manager who uses the ones abilities each day. They is probably inclined to offer you pointers and even a few fingers-on training.

3. Get an internship. Internships aren't only for college students and latest graduates. Many businesses are open to website hosting interns of any age who are willing to analyze and make a contribution to their business. Internships are designed to give you arms-on experience in a selected discipline. They will let you paintings alongside experts who've some of the competencies you're trying to achieve. If you attended college, your college's career offerings department could connect you

with internship opportunities. You can also attain out to people you already know who paintings in positions that require your favored competencies. They is probably inclined to install an awesome word and assist set up an internship for you.

4. Create a self-take a look at software. Thanks to libraries, bookstores, web sites and online guides, you've got tons of expert-degree understanding at your disposal. Make a plan to set apart some time each week to focus on learning about your preferred competencies. You can search for meetings or other occasions which might be coming to your vicinity. Neighborhood colleges and universities often host talks which are open to the public. You might discover an event that relates to the skills you're reading, and plenty of audio system are open to sharing their tips and advice with someone who is attempting to go into their field.

Key takeaway: there are several methods to develop your ability set, consisting of analyzing books, taking an internet training route and getting on-the-job education. Staying beforehand of the curve *when you're selecting new competencies to examine, examine the state-of-the-art trends and determine a way to live applicable to meet changing enterprise demands. As you pass about learning new talents, try to cognizance on areas you discover thrilling. You're much more likely to stay inspired to complete that programming or search engine optimization path if you have already got some curiosity about the concern. With some dedication and strength of mind, you may begin gaining key talents to help you stand out to employers.*

3

# How to get a job fast with no experience

Getting a job shortly appears as if a ambitious assignment, specially for the cause that time-to-rent can take as lengthy as 4 weeks. Long hiring methods can go away many challenge seekers tons much less than positive whilst in search of out a new career. If you're searching to make a cross soon, you can surprise if there's some thing you can do to hurry up the extended method. There definitely is, so we've compiled a listing of 20 pointers you may want to leverage to get a system rapid. From refining your resume to the interview observe-up, these strategies will help you find out the job you choose and get employed quickly. See for yourself:

1. Get specific with your undertaking search. It gradual is precious, even extra so at the same time as your purpose is to get a recreation speedy. Don't waste it through filling out a bunch of applications for positions you are most high-quality semi-interested by. Alternatively, make the effort to analyze positions you may actually experience, after which

use it gradual accurately to locate and study for positions that healthy what you're looking for out. Maximum method boards and recruiting net websites allow you to make particular searches primarily based definitely on your criteria, which consist of the identify of the placement, earnings, qualifications, and different requirements. Write out some key phrases that wholesome job obligations and your preceding work revel in so you can use every sites' are seeking for functionality efficiently and in your gain. Those centered searches additionally can assist you get rid of jobs that don't meet your necessities when it comes to region, revel in level, and different non-negotiable standards. The effects will supply you to accessible positions masses greater intently aligned collectively with your wishes. When you've decided jobs that suit, filling out functions ought to be a extraordinary deal a whole lot much less tedious than whilst you're making use of for positions that are now not a outstanding in shape.

2. Don't take delivery of a much less than ideal match. Don't compromise on what you fee most when it comes to in which you want to work. A job posting may additionally sound like a extraordinarily correct in structure to your abilties, however the business enterprise subculture needs to be a fit for you, too. Studies enterprise agency producers on-line, study employee opinions and speak subculture healthy in mobile phone displays to make positive that every the positions and the businesses you recollect healthy your artwork values and wishes. Earlier than establishing your studies, attempt compiling a list of what makes a business enterprise a amazing swimsuit for you: its venture, vision, and values; area or far off artwork options; organization-hosted activities; a collaborative surroundings;

and any different critical traits.

3. Don't end your search too quick. You've carried out your research and submitted your utility, resume, and cowl letter, however now what?  Preserve your eyes open for different capacity employers and possibilities as they flip out to be reachable — it's higher to use for severa positions that hobby you, as adverse to relying on one or packages turning into procedure offers.  If a business enterprise sends a rejection letter, take this opportunity to invite them what you may additionally have performed otherwise to be considered, and use any remarks to decorate future applications and interviews.

4. Write tailored cowl letters.  Cover letters are no longer a thing of the beyond: 87% of hiring professionals referred to they examine cowl letters. Even greater convincingly, tailor-made cowl letters elevated interviews with the useful resource of 51% and callback charges by way of way of 31%. It's high-quality exercise to alternate the quilt letter for every function you observe for, and that statistic proves that the try can pay off.  Supply a quick summary of your qualifications, provide concrete examples of your successes, and talk about how your knowledge will aid the employer thrive. Hiring managers want to recognize what units you different than exclusive applicants, so use your cowl letter to spotlight how your specific brain set makes you an exceptional in shape.

5. Make your resume activity-unique.  Much like your cowl letter, each resume you put up want to recognition on that specific job.  Be positive to spotlight your abilities and trip which would possibly be most really useful to that role, mainly

these which are listed inside the job description itself. With out citing your qualifications, your resume is possibly left out by means of an applicant monitoring machine or the hiring supervisor, and you may additionally be disqualified for the venture before than a character sees your utility. Leave out capabilities and ride that are now not relevant to the place you're making use of for so that you have room for what does.

6. Keep it easy and relevant. If you have pages and pages of enjoy, is it crucial to listing all of it? Now now not quite. In relation to pointing out your revel in and work history, hold it effortless and applicable. Summarize your past work journey succinctly and make certain descriptions of your procedure obligations are applicable to the placement you're making use of for. Forty% of hiring managers spend much less than a minute reviewing your resume, so make positive to make it count number with abilities and revel in that are applicable to the open role.

7. Employment isn't the complete lot on a properly-rounded resume. Many procedure seekers skip weeks or even months with out discovering the ideal task. This leaves gaps internal the work records area which may want to go away recruiters worried the manner seeker isn't dependable. Thankfully, mentioning your artwork documents isn't all there is to a resume. Make positive to function any volunteer paintings, persevering with education, or freelance initiatives you likely did for the length of the space. If you have been a stay-at-domestic figure, point out that as nicely. Recruiters choose to recognize what you had been doing and how you have been developing your capabilities whilst you weren't strolling for a

organization.

8.Get dressed the thing — in man or girl and on video. Maximum have heard the pronouncing, "get dressed for the venture you want, no longer the endeavor you have got." nicely, it sincerely does hold some reality. While going into an interview, don't costume simply for your component, costume for the a phase of pinnacle or senior control, or the role that you hope to accumulate in the route of your profession at the organization. This though applies inner the international of put up-pandemic recruiting: simply due to the reality your interview is via video chat doesn't imply you want to omit out on a specialist outfit. First impressions are the complete lot, especially even as you handiest have 30 minutes or so to discuss with any individual earlier than they decide to hire you. So, in case you want to get the assignment fast, make the main affect matter!

9. Don't pretend your skills. When it comes time for the interview, employers can inform whilst you're faking your skills and your way of existence in shape. They want to recognize who they're hiring and additionally you want to wholesome the function and tradition. Being deceptive permits neither of you, and can end result in horrific job placement, horrible average performance, and in the end, beginning your challenge search all as soon as more. There's no factor in getting a mission fast in case you quit up again at rectangular one in some short months. Saying what you suppose the company desires to hear would possibly get you the project alternatively at the value of your personal career increase and your relationship with that company. Being truthful is the magnificent way to exhibit off your abilities and land the venture of your dreams.

10.  Percentage your story and experiences.  Even as in the interview, it's imperative to returned up your abilities and revel in with concrete examples. Percentage memories about successes and gaining information of studies, and supply examples of duties and conditions at work that absolutely made your abilities stand out. Display how your skills helped benefit your final business enterprise with numbers, simply like the vary of leads closed, tickets resolved, or merchandise made. Use jargon and language that suggests your diploma of knowledge for your discipline.

11. Go away the negativity at the door. While you're speakme about previous testimonies and situations, it's imperative to take into account that you ought to now now not discuss down a past organisation.  Talking badly about human beings you used to artwork for makes the interviewer question what you may also have to point out about them down the road. This will create a lousy impact on your person. Plus, this is an interview about transferring ahead. Any previous discrepancies shouldn't intervene with your subsequent position.

12. Comply with up with the hiring manager. Whether you've heard once more about the exercise or not, it's indispensable to comply with up with the hiring supervisor or hiring crew after the interview. Ship a thank you letter or email mentioning the way it grow to be a pleasure to communicate with them and that you truly apprehend the possibility. Reiterate any thinking about why you're the high-quality in form for the position, and be positive to affirm your touch statistics and invite them to ask any in a similar fashion questions to useful resource their choice. This suggests that you are engaged and invested, and

your straightforward interest interior the position permit you to get employed fast.

13. Leverage your neighborhood to discover new possibilities. Occasionally, method probabilities spring from no longer possibly locations and stunning connections. Be open to speaking and networking with others on your subject. Whether at an business enterprise occasion, over e-mail, or over social media systems like linkedin, make it a factor to join to colleagues, classmates, and others for your company to keep a furnish for manner possibilities and occupation amplify sources.

14. Create a listing of reliable references. Earlier than making use of to any task, create a record of references and attain out to the ones human beings to make certain they might also be at ease with being listed as one amongst your references. Supply them a heads up that you are making use of to nice corporations which can contact them, too. Those ought to be these who understand you thru networking, previous co-people, or all and sundry else who can discuss on your art work experience and competencies. Make certain to choose references who're an tremendous supply of statistics. Pick human beings who are acquainted alongside with your artwork fashion and former projects, and who can provide an unbiased, honest opinion.

15. Apply more than as quickly as if it feels right. So, you utilized for a method and didn't get it. A few weeks later, you observe that the area continues to be open. Experience free to strive again! Take be aware of something that may want to have lengthy long gone mistaken the principal time and take some different crack at it with a revised resume and cowl letter. This

suggests initiative and your functionality to boost and develop.

16.   Flip your weaknesses into strengths.  All of us have weaknesses, and employers prefer to recognize about them. Recollect, a susceptible factor can additionally be one in all your strengths. For instance, your weak spot may be procrastination. But, however that, you continuously make the time limits and can produce extremely good paintings, even on speedy timelines. The equal can ignore for many different weaknesses. Anything your downfalls can be, use them in your gain and show that even although you're no longer best, you already comprehend the way to artwork thru your weaknesses and accomplish awesome paintings.

17.  Attention on your achievements.  Acknowledging your accomplishments is a first price way to expose what you're in a position to and the way you've already succeeded in your career.  You may also now not have 10 years of experience, however if you should show that your group doubled its income in 365 days, which can make a massive distinction whilst you're being taken into consideration for a function  While checklist your achievements, don't forget to embody any awards or certifications you've earned in your area.

18. Stand out from the rest with one-of-a-type details. Status out from different candidates is viable in severa approaches, from showcasing a internet work portfolio to sending in a presentation that acts as your cowl letter. These unique actions will assist employers and hiring managers take into account you and your work. Try an attractive tactic whilst additionally showcasing the unique abilities the employer is looking out out

correctly.

19. Exercise guaranteed physique language. Projecting self assurance in a challenge interview may also be the difference amongst being the 2d choice and getting the procedure fast. With sixty five% of notification going on nonverbally, assured physique language is every bit as integral as giving certain answers. Whether your interview is in character or on video, exercising your nonverbal conversation as heaps as you work-out your solutions to interview questions. Keep away from fidgeting, pay interest to your posture, and keep consistent eye contact for a assured demeanor. Employers want to recognize which you are assured in your capabilities and yourself. If you don't exhibit it, you should supply the influence that you aren't licensed for the location.

20. Be engaged with the interviewer. Hiring managers and employers desire to apprehend that you are listening and fascinated via what they've to mention. Ask questions and don't be afraid to point out you're undecided of an reply —it's nevertheless viable to have a exceptional interview even in case you don't apprehend the entire thing. It is in a position to even reassure recruiters that you're as it need to be representing your abilities in vicinity of really looking for to get the procedure quick. One of the excellent approaches to disclose you're engaged and interested is by way of way of being proactive. Browse the organisation's net site, examine evaluations, scroll via social pages, and lookup their enterprise undertaking, imaginitive and prescient, and values. Convey notes out of your lookup at the enterprise on your interview. This data will supply you thoughts for questions to ask your interviewer and

will exhibit the hiring crew you are assured and serious about the placement. Inside the publish-pandemic brain market, it is a ways plausible to get a venture quick, in precise in case you make an effort to prepare. There's no longer some thing greater incredible than a candidate who suggests up organized, confident, and organized to tackle any boundaries ahead. Positioned these 20 hints and your statistics of the competencies panorama to proper use to discover a position that matches your skills, and get employed rapid. If you are an hr or recruiting practitioner looking out out guidelines on the way to streamline and modernize your hiring strategies to acquire more pinnacle skills, join in our weblog these days for increased guidelines! Preserve studying for greater on navigating the cutting-edge nation of recruitment and hiring:

five things hr leaders want to do to put together for submit-pandemic recruitment

- recruiting pinnacle brain inside the midst of understanding shortage
- how hr managers are tackling new lease onboarding
- why you have to use candidate monitoring equipment

# 4

# What to Do When You Can't Find a Job

Sometimes when you're in the midst of a job search and you've been giving it your all, no matter your pleasant efforts, you simply can't discover a job.

It can be disheartening now not to see outcomes from all your tough work, however don't despair. By following a few easy hints when you can't discover a job, you can flip your job search into a success!

Note:

Consider These thirteen Tips

1. Take a Break

You don't want to stop your job search entirely, or even take a months-long hiatus, in order to supply your self a wreck from job searching. Even taking simply a day off each now and then can recharge your batteries so you'll sense geared up to leap lower back in, refreshed and prepared to go.

"It's OK to take some time off from your job search as soon as in a while. Allow your self a day or a few days off and spend that time doing some thing that energizes you and makes you happy, and mirror on what's going nicely in your search," . "Afterwards, you'll locate you'll be capable to get again to your job search with a renewed feel of strength and purpose."

## 2. Go Where the Jobs Are

Some human beings will cross to a specific city, state, or united states to locate a job in their field. But if you're searching for a faraway job, your area may additionally now not be a great factor. It does, however, assist to goal your search to the fields and jobs that are most well matched with faraway work. "Do a bit of lookup on who usually hires in your discipline to assist velocity alongside your search," .

## 3. Spruce up Your Online Presence

Studies have proven that the majority of hiring managers will seem to be at a person's on-line presence even earlier than attaining out to them for a job interview. How do your social media profiles look? Are they a mishmash of (public) household pictures and some political point-of-view posts? One of the most vital components of your job search is to make certain that your on line presence is up to date and professional.

Take the time to easy up your profiles, or create some new ones that exhibit you in a expert light, and maintain them modern-day so viable bosses can see that you're energetic on social media…for all the proper reasons.

## 4. Get Skilled or Schooled—or Both

If you're discovering that you aren't completely certified for the positions you've been making use of to, that ought to be one motive you can't locate a job. Employers regularly won't rent any individual who doesn't have the majority of the skills, education, or job ride imperative for the position. If you want to improve your talent set to be extra in line with what agencies are searching for, think about going again to college or discovering on line sources to obtain the abilities you need.

5. Change Your Mindset

It's convenient to sense defeated if you've been job looking for a lengthy time and now not getting any responses. If this is the case, a trade in standpoint may additionally be all you want to flip the nook and locate some success. "Just like taking a smash from your job search is important, so is having the proper mindset. It is tough to be a job seeker, making use of for many jobs and per chance no longer listening to lower back from employers,"

Instead of going into every new job search with trepidation, strive to remain high quality and see each and every utility as a danger to fine-tune and ideal your process.

"Work to focal point on the growth you are making with every application—honing your search tactics, getting environment friendly with your software process, and perception what key phrases to use for an ATS are all necessary equipment to use as you go via your search," . "Each time you follow for a job, you are enhancing your process, and that's exceptional development to touchdown a job. Celebrate these small steps!"

6. Try a Temporary Job

If you've been job looking for a whilst and nevertheless

haven't landed the ideal position, you may additionally desire to think about taking on a transient job. Temp jobs are an brilliant way to get your foot in the door at a company, analyze some new skills, and construct your expert network. And you by no means know, some temp workers, even these who are seasonal, are presented everlasting positions as soon as their unique mission ends.

## 7. Build Your Network

Especially if you're introverted, it can sense tough to put your self out there to develop your network. But networking is one of the first-class methods to meet new humans and generate leads that can assist with your job search. While most in-person networking occasions are on preserve throughout the pandemic, there are many on-line networking activities you can do from the remedy of your domestic workplace that can yield some notable results.

## 8. Review Your Resume

If you've been searching in your discipline and are certified for the positions you're making use of for however nevertheless can't discover a job, resume errors and typos can also be to blame. When you've examine (and reread) your resume so often, it's extra probably you'll omit some good sized issues.

"It's continually a awesome thought to have anyone else evaluate your resume earlier than you publish it. A spouse, household member, friend, or resume evaluation specialist can seem at your record with a clean set of eyes and let you recognize if there are any evident errors to right earlier than making use of for a job. If that's now not an option, strive altering the resume font,

font size, and font colour and then rereading your resume so it appears unique to you. Then, when you are satisfied, alternate it again to the proper font earlier than applying,"

## 9. Customize Your Application

When you're making use of to a couple of positions over the route of a few days, weeks, or months, it can be tempting to use the identical resume and cowl letter over and over once more with simply a few small tweaks right here and there. However, employers are searching for candidates who are the best fit, so taking the time to customise your resume and cowl letter to every job will assist you stand out from the crowd.

Keep in thought that one motive you can't discover a job may also be due to the fact the applicant monitoring gadget (ATS) isn't choosing up your facts based totally on its keyword searches. Customizing your resume and cowl letter to encompass applicable key phrases that the ATS has been programmed to appear for can supply you a leg up in the utility process.

## 10. Consider Other Industries

It may not be precisely what you desire initially, however if you've tried to locate a job in one enterprise and aren't having any luck, it may be time to seem at jobs in different fields. You can also find out you experience a new profession subject a good deal greater than you notion you would, and you'd be amazed how many of your capabilities are transferable from one discipline to another. Once you've made the switch, you may also even discover that a profession trade is an interesting and transformational time in your professional life!

## 11. Look for Other Types of Flexible Work Arrangements

You would possibly have your coronary heart set on working from domestic full-time with bendy hours, however that can also no longer be in the cards…for now. Thankfully, there are many kinds of bendy jobs beneath the huge banner of work flexibility. Expand your search to part-time jobs, freelance or contract gigs, bendy schedules, choice schedules, partial faraway work, or any mixture of those. Being open to different kinds of flexibility can lead you to job openings you may additionally no longer have observed if you have been solely looking out for full-time, a hundred percent far flung jobs.

## 12. Practice Your Interviewing Skills

If you've made it to the interview stage in the utility process, congratulations! But if these interviews aren't main to any job offers, it may also be time to improve your interviewing skills. You can exercise with friends, family, or even fellow job seekers who may be capable to provide pointers on what you're doing proper and the place you would possibly want some improvement.

If you have a profession mentor or a former boss who you're pleasant with, ask if they can do a mock interview with you, too. If not, you may additionally prefer to reflect onconsideration on on line profession teaching as an alternative to get optimistic and actionable feedback. With most interviews going on on-line these days, it's additionally useful to put together for the far flung interview manner to set your self up for success.

## 13. Pinpoint the Problem

If you can't locate a job, it's beneficial to take some time to look at why (and where) you can also be struggling. What phase of the job search system is giving you the most trouble? Is it that you can't locate jobs that you choose to follow to? Or do you no longer hear returned from employers after submitting your application? Are you getting to the interview stage and then getting handed over for positions? Understanding why you can't locate a job is an quintessential route towards correcting your path and touchdown your dream position!

For example, if you constantly conflict to discover best jobs in your industry, it may be that you're searching in the incorrect places. Big-box job search web sites provide a lot of positions, however the good sized majority can also no longer observe to you, your qualifications, or your bendy work needs. If you're searching for a work-from-home job, a area of interest website online will assist you discover positions that are greater centered to your goals.

If you're now not getting invited to interview, reflect on consideration on if your utility is the great it can be. Make certain that your resume has a modern-day structure and consists of applicable work trip to the job you're making use of to. If you're interviewing with hiring managers and no longer touchdown the job, are your interviewing abilities rusty, or are you not sure of how to promote your self throughout an interview? Practice can assist you work out the kinks so that you can get employed for the job you want.

# 5

# how to be mentally prepared for job interview?

We've all heard the cliché that "attitude is everything." But if you are a job-seeker getting prepared for an interview, it is extra than an empty phrase: It's a integral issue of your profitable preparation.

Until these days Aditya, a 43-year-old skilled Admin, had been out of work for over a yr due to a organisation downsizing. He confronted the equal predicament as many older job-seekers: He hadn't interviewed for a job in decades. The panorama seemed daunting.

He employed a profession counselor, polished up his résumé and lined up a promising job interview. Through mock interviews, he designed a approach that targeted on positivity and emphasised the values and capabilities he should contribute. When the time got here to interview, he stored the dialogue upbeat, successfully highlighting his job-related accomplishments. He landed the job and is returned to work full time.

"My instruction helped me method my interview with a calm, assured and nice demeanor," Aditya says.

Staying high quality all the time may also no longer be realistic, however too a great deal negativity can clearly damage your chances. If you take the time to prepare, you may existing the most relaxed, centered and assured model of yourself. Here are six approaches to be positive you are at your nice for your subsequent interview.

1. Give serious thinking to your tough and gentle skills.

Review your top, job-related strengths, and be equipped to emphasize technical or purposeful capabilities such as account management, commercial enterprise development, income support, venture administration or workforce supervision. Soft abilities — private attributes special to you that will set you aside from different job candidates — additionally assist you work successfully with different people. Use phrases such as "adaptable," "collaborative," "resourceful," "intuitive," "influential" and "cost-conscious." Think about them frequently so that when you are asked, "What abilities would you deem most necessary in this position?" you will now not solely have the reply at your fingertips, you will sound self-assured.

2. Think about your pinnacle accomplishments.

This requires inserting pen to paper first and cautiously selecting key success testimonies possibly to resonate with manageable employers. If you have difficulties organizing your accomplishments, strive questioning about them in phrases of problem, motion and cease result.

3. Invest some time and work with a profession coach.

You'll have to pay for the service, however mock interviews grant effective preparation. Consider them intellectual work-out routines for your confidence. Just as importantly, you will be uncovering hassle areas, nailing down key strengths and skills, and reviewing profession successes. And you will higher assume questions that the interviewer would possibly ask about your employment records and different considerations.

4. Put your self in the interviewer's shoes.

Imagine that whilst you are talking, the interviewer appears a long way away or uninterested. You can experience your probability to promote your self fading. Recognize the moment, and change gears — suppose about what questions you would ask a attainable worker if the tables have been turned. This shift in point of view isn't always easy, however it will assist you to be extra compelling and succinct and maybe re-light the interviewer's interest.

5. Manage your stress.

This is huge. Plan so that you can put together a calm, positively energized surroundings for your self the morning of your interview. Try to restriction undesirable distractions that day, and if you are very nervous, use deep- respiratory methods or meditation to decrease nervousness stages (just do not fall asleep!). One extra gorgeous way to decrease stress is very simple: Don't be counted on your GPS the day of the interview.

MapQuest or Google the agency tackle in advance of time (be positive to thing in rush-hour site visitors if you have an early-morning appointment). Plan to arrive 20 minutes early, and take 10 of these minutes to provide your self a pep discuss and arrange your ideas earlier than going inside.

6. Picture your self in the job.

This workout can be finished any time at some stage in your job search. Find a quiet spot, get cosy and shut your eyes. Visualize your self in the job you want. See your self sitting at your desk, speaking with your coworkers, working with your team. Envision your self being happy! This kind of nice visualization exercise is wonderful and can increase self belief and candor in the course of the interview process.

6

# 4 mind tricks to ace your next interview

Job interviews are a traumatic state of affairs the place the stakes are excessive for you to supply and impress. When you're on facet in these make-or-break scenarios, it's all too effortless to put your talent on autopilot and blurt out unrelated nonsense that may additionally have your interviewer scooting away.

To forestall that, we rounded up some of the satisfactory psychological thought hints to get you in the assured and organized headspace you want to ace an interview:

1) Act like you've already gotten the job

To act confident, you want to visualize the end line and embody the coronary heart and soul of a winner. That's the approach Capital One human assets govt Meghan Welch instructed Business Insider profitable candidates have used.

It helps if you've achieved the legwork to lower back this self assurance up. Acting like you've obtained the job ability you have options to questions interviewers deliver up. That potential making ready previously on questions interviewers can ask you, asking your pals to do mock interviews with you, and studying up on the organization itself. When you're that prepared, it will come thru in your physique language.

When you're performing as if you already have the role, your interviewers begin to see you as a colleague greater than one extra candidate. For interviewers, Welch stated this power comes off as: "I am notable excited about the hassle you are speaking about proper now and I have a total bunch of methods I would love to remedy it."

Of course, you favor to channel the strength of a profitable job applicant, however you don't favor to go overboard with it and pass the line into cocky delusion by way of telling your interviewer: "See you Monday!"

2) Hire-me physique language capability mirroring your interviewer

How you supply statistics can be as revealing as the records itself. Fidgeting hands, drumming fingers, and flailing gestures do now not deliver hire-me vibes, they expose your nerves. One of the easiest social cues to amplify your hiring probabilities is making normal eye contact with your interviewer. Body language specialists have discovered that when any person appears you in the eye, it suggests confidence, authority, and presence.

Maintaining eye contact is primary physique language knowledge. A greater superior type to take is consciously mirroring the tone, posture, mannerisms, and electricity of your interviewer. Social psychologists name this the "chameleon effect" and have located that the mirroring will increase your interviewer's possibilities of liking you and smooths over interactions.

So when your interviewer leans back, you lean back, too — however subtly. (You don't prefer to seem to be like an proper mime.)

3) Match what you wear to what you desire to project

The hues of what you put on to the interview sign what sort of character you are earlier than you even open your mouth. A 2013 CareerBuilder survey of 2,000 hiring managers and human sources gurus located that colorings act as temper rings — and blue was once the excellent shade you ought to put on to seem to be professional.

Here are the features the managers in the survey related with every color:

- Black: Leadership

- Blue: Team Player

- Gray: Analytical

- White: Organized

- Brown: Dependable

- Red: Power

- Orange: Creativity

Although orange alerts creativity, it used to be additionally the colour least preferred via managers, with one in 4 reporting that it appeared unprofessional.

4) Be yourself

You prefer to use these psychological hints to decorate the traits you already have — interviewers can inform when you're being phony, and you'll be penalized for it. A 2017 find out about posted in the Journal of Applied Psychology located that candidates who have a sturdy pressure to self-verify and existing themselves authentically have a greater possibility of success.

"In a job interview, we regularly attempt to existing ourselves as perfect. Our find out about proves this intuition wrong," the study's lead writer Dr. Celia Moore said. "Interviewers pick out an overly polished self-representation as inauthentic and probably mis-representative. But ultimately, if you are a wonderful candidate, you can be your self on the job market. You can be straightforward and authentic. And if you are, you will be extra possibly to get a job."

7

# Interview Psychology: How to Prepare Mentally

Preparing for a job interview in any circumstance requires a lot of foresight and forward-thinking; many carefree candidates have taken the liberty of turning up to an arranged interview except a pre-set 'game plan' and failed miserably when questions or duties occur that they did no longer expect.

Taking the time to sketch some pre-emptive measures such as lookup and gathering qualification certificates can make a large distinction in your overall performance in job interviews, and additionally permit you to make a effective and lasting influence on the interviewers themselves. So with this in mind, let's seem at a few tried and examined systems that can enhance your confidence, sharpen up your CV and make you stand out from the crowd.

Curriculum Vitae

Revising and sculpting your CV to go well with every man or woman job utility will assist you in a quantity of ways; firstly, it will make your CV extra attractive and in particular well-suited to every job function in question, it will make for a exquisite conversational piece in interviews and lastly, it might also assist to point out (or even provoke) which questions you can anticipate to hear in the interview.

When revising your CV, take into consideration the trip and skills you have, and choose which components of every practice to that job role. Going into extra element about positive components of previous job roles can also no longer appear like a large deal to you, however it will spotlight the key aspects of your ride that potential employers are searching for.

For example, if an applicant has journey in retail or hospitality and is searching to follow for jobs in administration then they would virtually have to spotlight the key areas of their preceding journey to exhibit they are an perfect candidate for the job. If the candidate had been to element the intricacies of their organizational skills, patron provider expertise, phone manner, and competency with computer systems then they would stand out as a greater appropriate candidate than they would have previously. The key to remodeling a CV is to pick out out key components of your preceding journey and skills and element them comprehensively to exhibit how well-suited to every job function you are.

The Interview

A awesome way of being psychologically organized for a job interview is to sense assured in your capability to reply the questions that are probably in advance of you; this can also appear a little obvious, however many humans go about it the incorrect way. Avoid rehearsing questions that you assume to come up with; instead, lookup the company, who they are, and what they do; this will supply you a excellent indication of what you will want to understand and enable you to come up with a few questions of your own.

If you have sourced job purposes from on line vacancies or on-line recruitment businesses then going that greater mile to locate out as a lot as feasible about your prospective employers is a must; a easy digital advert will supply solely a short description of the job position and you have to appear into the business enterprise and its products/services to find out precisely what your job function would be.

There are positive matters all potential employers are searching for in interviews, some extra apparent than others. It goes barring announcing that interviewers are genuinely search-ing for the most equipped candidate possible, however an enthusiastic candidate who is inclined to supply 110% to the corporation is an awful lot greater pleasing than an equally certified candidate with no enthusiasm or 'drive'. Coming throughout as an enthusiastic and keen candidate is simpler than you may additionally think; by way of asking the proper questions and adopting the proper attitude, it's pretty easy to come throughout as a vibrant and likable person.

Often interviewers like to ask: "Where do you see your self in 'X' years' time?" and many candidates would oftentimes reply with an overconfident and unrealistic reply such as "I'd like to be a manager" or "I'd like to be head of my department".

Interviewers love modesty alongside competence and answering questions with modest solutions which exhibit you are nonetheless hardworking and ambitious, but do no longer overestimate your skills is a a good deal greater eye-catching quality. An reply alongside the strains of "I accept as true with that if I proceed to increase my abilities and examine as lots as feasible from my friends then these possibilities will existing themselves in time" is a good deal greater effective. Obviously, it's smart to put your very own character and spin on this template mindset however discovering the comfortable medium between modesty and ambitiousness is an desirable pleasant indeed.

Upon the interview, you will probably have an possibility to ask any questions you can also have about the employer or the job role; this is a splendid hazard to exhibit that you have finished your homework and researched the company. Mention sure merchandise or services the agency gives and ask for finer small print surrounding them, and surely ask if there are any steps you can take to higher put together for the job function simply in case they figure out to provide you a call.

Conclusion

So there you are, some key hints to assist you higher put together for job interviews and applications. Remember, do your homework and act with modesty, and your competence and likability will shine through!

8

# Your LinkedIn Network Can Help You Land Your Next Job

Whether you're simply getting began in your career, searching to make a pivot, or are a professional expert looking for a new job, the nice human beings to lean on for guide are the human beings you know. Members like you have been 4x extra probable to get employed when they leveraged their networks on LinkedIn whilst job seeking.

Starting these conversations can be nerve-wrecking though, in particular if it's been a whilst when you consider that you closing spoke. To assist you overcome any anxiousness and encourage that first step, right here are a few pointers and dialog starters to strive out:

Identify the humans you be aware of

Your social acquaintances, alumni, and former colleagues are excellent humans to join with on LinkedIn. Once they're in your network, you can ship them a LinkedIn message to seize up and see how they're doing. Keeping the relationship sparkling makes it less complicated to attain out the subsequent time you want profession recommendation or a job referral.

Interested in becoming a member of a precise employer or pursuing a unique role? Use search to filter your connections based totally on their companies, industries, and job functions. You can additionally see whether or not you have any connections who work at a unique enterprise from a company's web page or job listing.

LinkedIn Home Page
    Start a significant conversation

Networking is all about constructing relationships thru true conversations. If it's been a whilst considering the fact that you've reached out to your connection, lead with curiosity through checking their profile and current undertaking to see the today's traits in their career. Use that as thought to get the dialog going with a LinkedIn message.

Here's an example:

"Hi Sarah, I can't accept as true with it's been two years on account that we final caught up. I seen you are now at {new company}. How has your transition been?"
    Ask for the assist you need

Depending on the stage of your job search, your community can be useful in a few special approaches - for profession advice, introductions to others, or a referral for a particular job. Once you're clear on your goal, grant context and any beneficial statistics that can empower your connection to assist you out.

Here's a few examples:

Ask for profession advice

"As I pursue [your profession goal], I'd love to research greater about [your question]. Given your heritage in [connection's credentials], I was once hoping to time table a 30-minute video chat with you. Would you be open to that?"
    Ask for an introduction

"I'm presently fascinated in pursuing [your subsequent role] and observed that you are linked to [mutual connection]. I'd admire an introduction so that I can study extra about [your question]."
    Ask for a referral

"I observed that your business enterprise is presently hiring for a [your subsequent role] and I'm involved in pursuing the opportunity. Do you idea referring me to the recruiter or hiring manager?"
    Invest in the relationship

The energy of your community relies upon on how properly you nurture your relationships over time. Be certain to follow-up via giving human beings updates on your job search, reporting again on how their recommendation labored for you, or sending a speedy thank you word and supplying your assist in return.

We've additionally made it handy for you to maintain the relationships clean as an alternative than simply achieving out when you want some thing specific. You can privately share applicable posts from your feed to spark a conversation, agenda espresso chats over video, or begin a crew dialog amongst a few humans you comprehend who share the equal interests.

These small steps can have a collectively really useful and advantageous influence inside your profession and community.

# 9

# How to Use LinkedIn to Get a Job?

Are you the using LinkedIn to its fullest to get a job?

I grew to become on the TV currently and noticed a "CBS This Morning" interview with Jeff Weiner, CEO of LinkedIn. Needless to say, it stimulated me to take a seat down and write. After all, I used to be receiving records on how to enhance your LinkedIn profile throughout a job search straight from the CEO's mouth, so I had to share.

Why must you use LinkedIn for your job search?

It's no secret that LinkedIn is the pinnacle expert social networking web page with 133 million customers in the U.S. on my own and achieving 200 nations and territories round the world. Per the Jobvite Recruiter Nation Survey, 87 percentage of recruiters use LinkedIn as section of their candidate search. As a expert or student, it is the famous location to community and appear for job opportunities; even former U.S. President Barack Obama as soon as joked throughout a TV press conference that he would be a part of

LinkedIn to assist him land a job after his time period was once up!

The trouble is that if you are solely updating your profile now and then, you are now not entirely utilising all LinkedIn can do for you, which consists of taking hours off of your job search. Below are some tactical recommendations on how you can leverage LinkedIn to its fullest to amplify your professional community and land your subsequent awesome job.

On CBS This Morning, LinkedIn's CEO cited the following three pointers to maximize the practicable of your LinkedIn profile:

Keep your profile up to date.

Be complete about contemporary competencies and objectives.

Highlight your latest experience.

When requested what used to be most vital about a candidate's profile and how to make the satisfactory use of the platform, Weiner replied that first and principal "authenticity" was once important.

"Be yourself, characterize who you are. It's no longer simply your experiences; this is no longer a resume … This is a greater dynamic strategy to representing your experiences, your skills, your objectives, what you know, what you are fascinated in inside a expert context," Weiner explained. "It's now not simply about the comprehensiveness; it is additionally about freshness of the information, and the greater entire and the greater fresh, the greater latest that that facts has been updated, the greater possibilities that are going to accrue to our members."

14 methods to use LinkedIn to get a job

In addition to Weiner's advice, I've introduced eleven extra moves you can take to leverage LinkedIn for most effectivity in securing your subsequent position. For the sake of this article, let's say your preferred agency that you simply cannot wait to work for is referred to as Gone Bananas. Follow these suggestions on how to leverage LinkedIn, and you will be an worker of Gone Bananas soon:

1. Keep your profile up to date. LinkedIn participants with a profile image are 14 instances extra possibly to get hold of web page views, whilst these who publish capabilities are thirteen instances greater probable to have profile views in contrast to these who don't, per LinkedIn's blog. There are greater than 45,000 capabilities to pick out from on LinkedIn to red meat up your profile, so if you prefer Gone Bananas to note you, make positive to frequently replace your profile, add a profile photo, and encompass your wonderful skills.

2. Be complete about present day abilities and objectives. To make certain you are the usage of LinkedIn to locate a job correctly, do not go away whatever out about your cutting-edge abilities and objectives. Use your headline to share your essential goal if it makes experience and add all of your capabilities to your page. You do not prefer it to appear like you have not up to date your web page in a while, as recruiters and organizations may pass by you through if it does.

3. Highlight latest experience. You choose your current ride evident to anybody who views your page, particularly when you are actively attractive with connections and corporations to land a job — which is the cause you are probable analyzing this post, after all.

4. Update your headline. Your photo, name, and headline (which is listed beneath your photo) are the solely gadgets human beings see when they do a search. Your headline need to stand out and spotlight what you do or what kind of role you are searching for. "HR expert connecting personnel with management" are examples of headlines that are clear and may clutch interest when in contrast to plain-Jane headlines like "Chemical engineer in the public sector."

5. Let human beings understand you are available. If you can announce the truth that you are searching for a job, do so. Use your headline to make the announcement. For example, "Writer searching for agencies in want of a pleasant ghost (or ghostwriter)" and "Petroleum engineer prepared to strike oil and make you rich" may trap a recruiter or hiring manager's attention.

6. Build your community to the 1st degree. Your connections can exponentially amplify your publicity and get entry to to different connections. LinkedIn makes it convenient to join with human beings you comprehend by using importing your contact lists from websites such as Gmail.

7. Research the businesses you are fascinated in and comply with them. LinkedIn makes it convenient throughout the job

hunt to locate and comply with companies. If you have not already achieved so, make a listing of the corporations you would like to work for and comply with them on LinkedIn. This will assist you continue to be in the recognize about organization information and new positions as they emerge as available.

8. Use the Advanced Search. Use LinkedIn's Advanced Search choice and do a search on your preferred companies. Find out who of your connections is related with Gone Bananas, for example, and make a list. You can attain out to these human beings relying on their connection with the company. If they work there, you can ask questions about the organisation culture. If they are a purchaser or carrier provider, you can ask what it is like to do commercial enterprise with them. Get innovative and have enjoyable doing your lookup so you can navigate how to excellent strategy the enterprise for a job when you are ready.

9. Ask for an introduction. Once you're prepared to attain out to Gone Bananas, you can ask your connection(s) to make an introduction to anybody they're linked to inside the organization.

10. Look for alumni related with your university or university. Doing a search for your university or college is a extraordinary way to join with alumni who went to the equal college as you. You can attain out to them and share this frequent hobby to assist you land your subsequent job.

"I would propose that one of the best, best approaches to

leverage the strength of LinkedIn is thru the usage of the Alumni tool. You can first be part of [or follow] your alumni university and then search for previous alumni at businesses or locations of employment you are involved in," she elaborated, "You additionally can enter any university and search to see how many levels of separation you may additionally be from alumni at any school."

11. Be greater than a wallflower. Be lively on LinkedIn, and as Weiner suggests, be genuine and current. Post any articles you write, movies you post, and so on, as updates. Get worried with agencies and have interaction with others on LinkedIn. The extra you have interaction and submit as a professional, the extra you may be seen and construct recognition.

12. Get concerned in LinkedIn Professional Groups. Do an Advanced Search to become aware of expert agencies in your location and get involved. This will assist increase your network, exhibit your understanding (when you have interaction in on-line conversations and reply questions that come up), and perhaps join you to the businesses you favor to work for in the future. When learning groups, you prefer to take part in organizations that have latest activity. Otherwise, you would possibly be losing your time if a crew would not have every day or everyday interplay online.

13. Research your future boss and govt team. Before going in for an interview, you can use LinkedIn to lookup hiring managers and interviewers to discover out about their likes, interests, and more. You can leverage this statistics for the duration of your interview to create relatability and exhibit

that you've got finished your homework.

14. Network after commercial enterprise hours. According to Mashable, information exhibit that solely 8.33 percentage of Americans use LinkedIn throughout working hours in contrast to other social media sites, such as Facebook (with nearly 30 percentage of human beings the use of it at some point of work hours), indicating that you may get extra interplay and publicity if you replace your status, network, and join with human beings and agencies after enterprise hours on LinkedIn. Test this out at special instances of the day to see what works quality in getting responses and different interactions.

# 10

# Actionable Tips For Creating Opportunities Now

How Do You Create Opportunities?

There are so many methods to create possibilities in the world, whether or not it is enhancing yourself, discovering deep and beneficial relationships, beginning your very own business, or getting promoted at work. From enhancing your monetary standing to deepening your expertise of the world and the humans round you, we have you covered.

Create Your Own Opportunities

I realized early on in lifestyles that I had to begin developing my personal possibilities due to the fact no one would supply me whatever if I did now not work for it. I had nothing, I used to be going to inherit nothing, and I had no one to provide me a hand. So, I commenced through analyzing and making sure I completed school. I went on to fund my personal University training whilst working. I realized I had one product, the product used to be me, and I had to get that product right.

But ample about me; it's all about inspiring you to make and take possibilities that will enrich your existence and these round you.

15 Ways To Create Life Opportunities
1. Be Mindful About What Happens Around You
Being aware is in actuality the act of perception what is going on round you at the current moment. Being considerate and reflective, searching at your existence nearly as an unbiased observer. Spend a little time every day to replicate upon the conditions you had been in, the things to do you undertook, and the humans you interacted with. Ask your self the following questions:

Are these the humans I desire to be with?
How did I deal with the conditions I was once in?
Did I operate any things to do that will in addition my cause?
Am I on the proper track?
Were there any possibilities I may additionally have missed?
The easy act of self-reflection and observance will assist set you on the proper path.

2. Reach Out & Harvest The Knowledge of Others
Trent Hankinson – Frontman and supervisor of the band Aqua Seca.

When I started out Aqua Seca, the choice was once no longer made completely with the aid of myself. In fact, I reached out to all of the human beings that I knew had know-how about tune and the track industry. I desired to seek advice from them to see if what I desired to do used to be even well worth doing.

After accomplishing out, I got here away with a ton of recommendation and severa telephone numbers to name further, so I did. To be fair, I acquired my unique recommendation of attaining out to human beings from Ray Dalio and his e book Principles. He says that you regularly are no longer the one who can make the nice choices for yourself, so it is excellent to attain out to human beings who are educated about the concern to inform you as to what the nice choice is.

This is now not always the most daring way to make possibilities for yourself, however it truely helped me. And Aqua Seca would no longer be the band that it is nowadays except his advice.

3. Surround Yourself The Right People

I grew up highly terrible in a terrible neighborhood; I had few possibilities and had a circle of buddies to match. My quality pals at college have been a properly bunch, however as we received to the a long time of sixteen to 18 years old, they commenced falling in with the incorrect people. Drugs, violence, and partying grew to be the weekend undertaking of choice.

The more moderen human beings that joined our social circle had been the sorts of human beings that noticed no probability in the world, they have been often unemployed via choice, and a few even went begging in the town throughout the day to get cash for alcohol; they begged even even though they did no longer have too. I reflected that this used to be no longer going to be my life, getting arrested for being in a bar brawl or for dealing drugs.

I labored so difficult academically that I was once supplied a vicinity at a University on the different facet of the country. I departed for University, and I left all of them behind. They visited occasionally, and when I used to be home, I met up with them, however it grew to be clear I was once no longer one of them anymore, I was once different, and they distanced themselves from me.

My University pals are like my brothers, pals for over 30 years; we lived together, traveled together, and constructed our lives together. They stimulated me to come to be something better, no longer by using words, by using their moves and companionship.

Surround your self with the proper humans for you, and the possibilities for tremendous friendships will flourish.

4. Travel & Broaden Your Experiences
   "TO TRAVEL IS TO EVOLVE." – PIERRE BERNARDO

I began journey travelling when I was once 20 years old, and I by no means honestly stopped. My first day trip was once to the USA, accompanied via Thailand and India in subsequent years. Everywhere I have been gave me some thing back, an insight, a treasured memory, or a high-quality story.

After my outing to India in 1990, I realized how completely happy humans ought to be, even even though they owned nothing. I additionally realized that I used to be so fortunate to be born in Europe; the distinction in poverty and hygiene stages used to be unbelievable.

Finally, I realized that the majority of the human beings in the world stay below the strain of corrupt dictatorships, severe poverty, and a serious lack of possibilities to enhance their situation.

I met humans whose travels actually modified their lives; they encountered possibilities to stay a extraordinary lifestyles and do specific things. I without a doubt met my future spouse whilst backpacking in Peru in South America. We hiked the Inca Trail collectively and had been in love ever since.

This may want to appear to you, but it genuinely will now not if you continue to be at home.

Telecommuting In To Work Across The Globe

5. Think of How Everything Can be Improved
   Some of the biggest possibilities are no longer outstanding new inventions; they are ordinarily iterative enhancements to current things. Consider the Dyson Vacuum Cleaner. Vacuum cleaners already existed. Still, Sir James Dyson figured he ought to enhance the sketch by way of putting off the annoyance of having to continuously purchase and change the bag. On this easy iterative improvement, he constructed the Dyson empire that disrupted an industry. Sir James went on to do it once more with the aid of growing the first useable cordless Dyson Vacuum cleaner. An enchancment on an already current invention. I personal one, it used to be exorbitantly expensive, however now we can smooth the complete residence in 10 minutes, as a substitute of hours.

Everything can be improved; the key is to locate matters that you can improve. The subsequent time you are aggravated by means of a product or service, suppose about what you would do to enhance it. Do this frequently enough, and your subsequent chance will be ready for you.

6. Think About a Service People Need.

I continuously assume about the jobs humans have to do due to the fact no one else will do it. Two years ago, it was once the center of summer, and the rubbish series had simply happened. It used to be our natural refuse, so the dustbin wanted to be cleaned due to the fact of the maggots and flies and the lousy smell. Now that is a job I hate doing.

I noted to a younger acquaintance I had that if they had been searching for freelance work, all they had to do used to be drop some leaflets in the nearby area, supplying to easy the refuse containers on series day. It would be two days per month, and they should cost $5 per bin. The younger chap is actually cleansing up.

Think about the jobs that humans hate. Think about how you can make cash out of it. From canine strolling to strain cleansing driveways, the possibilities are endless.

7. What Do You Do Better Than Most?

We are all excellent at something. Think about what you are appropriate at, typically what you excel at is some thing you enjoy. For some, it is writing, picture design, or coding.

Head on over to Upwork or Fiverr to see what lots of human

beings are doing to liberate possibilities and earn cash doing the matters they love.

What are you high-quality at?

8. People Love To Talk: Listen & Learn

It is so convenient to fall into the lure of speakme about yourself. I in my view have an inner alarm bell that sounds when I recognize that I have been the solely one speaking for the ultimate 10 minutes. Don't be the senseless talker, be the listener. Start conversations, ask questions, engage, however when you locate your self rambling on, be conscious it is time to let others specific themselves. I definitely have discovered a lot from actually listening to people. Also, by using listening, absolutely listening, and understanding, you can get the measure of a person.

During a conversation, ask your self these questions:

Do they say whatever of value?
    Do they speak about whatever meaningful?
    Do they attempt to be humorous?
    Can you do some thing for them?
    Can they assist you in any way?
    Do they have any actual pals or relationships?
    If the reply is yes, they might also be any individual to spend extra time with.

Try these ideas whilst in conversation:

Is the dialog compelled and shallow?

Do they bitch a lot?

Do they criticize others?

Do they leap to a terrible opinion?

Do they continuously right you and these round them?

Do they specific opinions that are towards your values?

If the reply is yes, you would possibly prefer to keep away from these people.

9. Build a Rapport Before You Self Promote

To release possibilities with others, you want to first construct a rapport.

Promoting one's abilities and competencies is herbal for all people who is in search of to hustle up new opportunities. But by no means make the cardinal mistake of beginning to hustle earlier than you have surely constructed any appreciation or vibe with any other person.

There is nothing worse than talking with any individual at a function. Suddenly, they have their enterprise card out and are forcing it into your hand; it simply leaves a bitter after style due to the fact you be aware of they solely spoke with you because you are a conceivable enterprise money-making opportunity.

The truth is that human beings solely do commercial enterprise with or assist human beings that that like and respect. So retailer your self-respect and dignity, solely try to pitch anyone when you assume they like and be aware of you sufficient to have confidence you and do commercial enterprise with you.

10. How to Win Friends & Influence People

103 Actionable Tips For Creating Opportunities Now Career & PromotionYes, Dale Carnegie was, and nevertheless is today, a exquisite idea for tens of millions of people.

When I used to be sixteen years old, besides any superb function mannequin in my lifestyles and missing direction, I became to this book. It may appear cliche, however this e book truely did exchange my life.

If you have no longer examine this book, do it now. Order it straight away and soak up the fantastic insights it lavishes on the mind.

But do no longer mistake the title "How to Win Friends & Influence People," it would possibly propose a low priced way to superficially manipulate humans for your personal purposes; this ought to no longer be similarly from the truth. This is a e book that teaches you super training in how to interact, construct significant relationships, and respectfully construct a circle of human beings round you that you love and that love you. It achieved all this while encouraging you to unleash your management skills.

11. Hire A Business / Career Coach

A certainly precise profession or commercial enterprise educate will have actual work commercial enterprise experience, commercial enterprise connections, and a association experience for the neighborhood enterprise environment. They can endorse you on startups, funding, and even profitable profession moves. The pleasant will additionally be capable to function workouts with you that can assist you reply questions about your self and your passions that you can't deduce with the aid of yourself.

There are a range of corporations on line that can furnish a faraway enterprise or profession coach. You can appear up any person regionally that you can sit down with face to face who is aware the neighborhood commercial enterprise local weather and has enterprise contacts. A accurate instruct can unencumber a wealth of opportunities.

12. Understand Your Core Values & Share
   Find Out What Your Values and Principles Are?
   If your work is aligned with your values, principles, and strengths, you will make bigger your ordinary delight with life. But how do you be aware of what your values are?

You ought to begin via answering the following easy questions:

What are your profession priorities? If you seem cautiously at your profession route so far, you will effortlessly be aware matters that are your priority. Take the time to suppose about the selections you made and make a listing of values that proceed to be repeated at every of your roles.

Do you favor to have greater freedom or a greater salary? If you have prevalent a suggestion for a decrease earnings that offers you greater freedom, then your moves exhibit that you fee your independence extra than monetary reward.

Do you opt for place of business flexibility, or do you revel in working in a busy office? Some human beings are tremendously social and consequently want the hustle and bustle of an workplace environment. Some select to work by myself on complicated troubles and experience the quiet time to focus.

Do you decide upon to work without delay with customers, or instead work in a back-office group in operations or inner projects? Is wining and eating purchasers and sealing offers your thing, or do you decide upon to force interior trade or tasks to enhance the enterprise throughout organizations?

What made you joyful when you had been younger? Children have the capacity to experience lifestyles in an harmless beauty, which alas fades with the growing responsibilities, expectations, and age. Take time to recall all the matters you absolutely loved as a child. What has made you happy, and then assume about what you virtually like now? With some creativity from your side, it is pretty feasible to discover a way to combine these things to do into your profession picks as an adult.

How do you spend your free time? The way you pick to spend your free time is pretty indicative of what you value. Choose an pastime that brings you the most pleasure and attempt to locate out which ingredient is most vital to you; is it speaking with people, assisting others, or gaining knowledge of new skills.

Share your plans. Trust your closest people, who will be sincere with you. Ask them what they suppose about your strengths and weaknesses. These conversations can make you see profession paths and possibilities that you in all likelihood have no longer regarded so far.

## 13. Be Trustworthy – Always

Honour, respect, and have faith are three matters you must stay by. You need to by no means betray the have confidence of others unless, of course, they are an ax murdering serial killer, then it's OK. Being considered as honest unlocks so many possible opportunities, be they friendships, partnerships, or insights. Being the rock capability you have the appreciate of others, and they will favor to assist and promote you besides you even having to ask.

## 103 Actionable Tips For Creating Opportunities Now Career & Promotion

## 14. Share A Little Humor, Especially Self Deprecating

The excellent praise you will ever get from a British individual is they will say you are a "good laugh." The British love humor; that does now not suggest they are all funny; it simply capability that even attempting receives you bonus points.

Inject a little humor into your interactions with people, and they will heat to you. I do no longer suggest telling jokes, simply attempting to see the lighter aspect of life. Also, if you can inform a few humorous tales with you at the butt stop of the joke, that will endear human beings to you.

Someone who can't snigger at themselves is anyone you don't prefer to know.

## 15. What is Your Elevator Pitch?

The elevator pitch is the potential to provide an explanation for your complete reason in the time it takes to inform anyone on an elevator, which ability about one minute.

My elevator pitch for greatworklife.com would be:

"Sharing with human beings how to acquire their model of greatness in their work and non-public life. Whether you prefer to be a leader, be your personal boss or really have outstanding private relationships, I desire to share my trip and that of others with the world?"

Take the time to assume of your elevator pitch; it would possibly be the solely aspect humans keep in mind of you.

5 Ways Education Creates Opportunity
   1. Expanding Your Mind Through Books.
   The improve from cave artwork to writing to the printing press used to be a brilliant pass for the protection of human knowledge, and regardless of the digital age, the written word, whether or not on a Kindle, on a blog, in a database, or in paperback, is nonetheless the best way of shooting and distributing knowledge.

Take benefit of the expertise of all humankind and examine a book; it will free up ideas and encourage you to launch possibilities that you by no means notion possible. You can begin with these two books.

103 Actionable Tips For Creating Opportunities Now Career & Promotion 103 Actionable Tips For Creating Opportunities Now Career & Promotion
   2. Optimize Your Learning Time With Audio Books

103 Actionable Tips For Creating Opportunities Now Career & Promotion

If you have a smartphone, you have the world's information at your fingertips except the want for a tree to be reduce down and barring the want to take a seat down and read.

Audiobooks are a superb way to soak up understanding when you do now not have time to sit down down and read. You can revel in audiobooks when driving, hiking, walking, and even when gardening.

I individually get thru at least 50 books per year, yes, really. I have tried many audiobook services, however for me, Audible by using Amazon is the satisfactory for rate and purchaser service.

3. Watch Documentaries – YouTube & Ted Talks

A easy search on YouTube for "entrepreneur documentaries" uncovers a wealth of fascinating and inspiring documentaries, from Elon Musk to Richard Branson. Another superb choice is to search for "Ted Talks Opportunities," which uncovers this Ted Talk.

4. Subscribe To Industry Journals

Whatever enterprise you presently work in or the enterprise you aspire to work in; you can advantage from enterprise periodicals and magazines. As an lively investor and commercial enterprise owner, I for my part subscribe to the Technical Analysis of Stocks & Commodities Magazine and the Economist Magazine. Such publications regularly spotlight key problems in the industry, notion leaders and can liberate possibilities in your mind. Interesting additionally are the adverts in enterprise journals, which can supply you thoughts about the opposition and how they pitch their services. In addition, thru the job postings, you see who is hiring and which groups are making waves.

## 5. Listen To Podcasts

The Podcast certainly took off in 2004 when Apple promoted it in conjunction with the iPods and iPhones. There are over 550,000 Podcasts available, whether or not you have an Apple or Android phone. There are Podcasts masking each and every subject matter imaginable, from investing to enterprise and career, and many of them are of top quality. Best of all, Podcasts are definitely free, so they are commonly backed with adverts.

You can head on over to Player. FM and have a appear around; on Android, I would propose the Podcast Republic App.

## 3 Examples of Serendipity Leading to Opportunities

### 1. Disasters Lead to Opportunities

Melissa Ong, founder of M&P International Freights, one of the pinnacle freight forwarders in Singapore

I used to be searching for new studying possibilities to improve myself with new skills. I got here throughout an e-commerce category and determined to locate out extra about it. The direction prices a bomb, however I determined to go beforehand simply to research some thing new.

The e-commerce type became out to be a hoax, and I did no longer study an awful lot from it. Nonetheless, I made some new pals who shared the identical values as me about learning. We had been in a position to hit it off and grew to be very proper friends.

Several months later, we commenced a few agencies collectively primarily based on our person competencies and comple-mented every different sincerely well. Today, we are high-quality commercial enterprise companions and have realized so a lot from every other. None of this would have occurred if I did now not go for the e-commerce category in the first place.

2. Do Something, Anything.

I have been working for the reason that the age of 13 and have by no means stopped. Here is a style of some of the jobs I had as a teenager:

I delivered milk on Sunday morning at three am
    Delivered newspapers, I hated it
    I labored in a Fish and Chip Shop, lousy odor and a worse boss; I give up after two weeks.
    Walked door to door promoting substitute windows, a absolutely terrible job, lasted 4 weeks.
    Worked in a video store, first-rate job ever for a 17-year-old
    Manager of the video store, even higher job for an 18-year-old
    Worked in a name middle promoting Cinema tickets
    Worked night time shift in a refrigerated warehouse slicing

veggies in Portland Oregon

While many of my college associates have been sitting round unemployed and no longer searching for work, I was once working. What did I get from this work? I realized there are a lot of crappy jobs. I realized there have been some handy jobs. I discovered a awesome smartphone manner; I realized how to pitch any individual a sale on their very own doorstep and discovered how to deal with the insults I received. Ultimately I realized having no greater training left me with solely low-paid jobs, and going to University was once one of the pleasant possibilities I have ever seized.

3. Experimentation Success For The Moose Poop Woman

How I have considered some abnormal matters in the world, however one of the most placing to me is the Moose Poop female Mary. She has actually created a enterprise on Etsy out of developing clocks, jewelry, and so a great deal extra out of Moose excretions.

There is no doubt Mary likes developing things, and this is a certain signal that humans will purchase anything. If you have a hobby, assume about how you can flip it into a business.

3 Steps to Expert Opportunities

1. Get Certified

The two foundations forming the foundation of any knowledge are certification and experience. Whatever expert work you pick out to undertake, you most in all likelihood will want to have some kind of certification.  Nearly each and every enterprise affords certifications, whether or not it is a Certified

Stock Market Analyst or a Wine Sommelier; your first stepping stone is a certification. A certification genuinely locations a rubber stamp on your knowledge; this offers humans self belief in your abilities. A amazing region to seem to be for certifications reachable in precise industries is CareerOneStop, which is subsidized by means of the US Department of Labor.

## 2. Build Experience

Your doable new customers, employees, or consumers will prefer to understand you can do the job; this capacity proving your experience. There are many internships and apprentice-ships handy to assist you construct experience. But what if the job you prefer to do, has no formal apprenticeship schemes? Try drawing close groups in your area of interest and provide to work for free. It may no longer appear realistic to work for no income, and we all want to earn, however you may want to strive it on a part-time basis, evenings or weekends.

If you virtually desire to spoil floor in a new area, you want to commit the proper time and effort; constructing your basis of certification and trip will set up you, and you will be prepared to propel your self forward.

what does a answer seem like

## 3. Answer Peoples Questions

If you are constructing trip in a new subject or even prefer to construct your expertise in an present subject in order to create new possibilities for yourself, strive this. Locate the applicable on line communities that have message boards and contribute. It will provide you the chance to examine from others, and even extra importantly, you can see what questions human beings ask and what wants and lack of know-how they have. You can even examine from these who whinge online, as humans who whinge typically are sad with the carrier or product; you can then suppose about the elevated offerings and merchandise that would meet their needs.

6 Ways Building Your Brand Created Opportunity

1. Start A Blog On Something You Love

I commenced a private finance blog, which now presents me with passive profits via affiliate marketing. This firstly started out as a aspect hustle, however the weblog has been growing to the factor whereby it is shut to equaling my profits I make as a CFP. I was once in a position to make use of my present client e mail database to develop the weblog and refer economic offerings that I propose to my clients. I used to be additionally in a position to leverage my current information base as a CFP and share that expertise with readers of my blog.

Blogging has been a extraordinary outlet for me to join with a wider audience, share my knowledge, and instruct others. At first, I didn't have any intentions to monetize my weblog and didn't comprehend the chance that used to be there proper in the front of me. I have additionally discovered it a terrific way to expand my publicity and strengthen my expert network, which has led to in addition opportunities.

Blogging is extraordinarily handy and requires nearly no funding capital to get started. Anyone can get began and share their know-how inside their niche.

2. LinkedIn The Business Opportunity Engine

LinkedIn is the expert enterprise community of preference for the western world. If you make an effort to whole your profile, add your work experience, certifications, and join to your colleagues, you will have the begin of a enterprise probability engine.

Ensure that your buddies and co-workers add evaluations of you and your capabilities to your profile. You can begin by way of endorsing these human beings first and asking them to return the favor. As this builds, you will locate you are contacted through competitor companies, recruiters, and even humans looking for your services. I even be aware of enterprise proprietors who do now not use an electronic mail listing anymore; they really use their LinkedIn contacts, as they get a good deal higher patron engagement via LinkedIn. You can even join to me on LinkedIn.

Social Networks = Opportunity?
Social Networks = Opportunity?
3. Building Your Brand – Twitter

For me, Twitter is like being in a soccer stadium and shouting your message alongside with 50,000 different fans. The possibilities you will get heard are very slim. Twitter is used quite through celebrities and the media, and these in search of to create a tribe/following. It can be sincerely challenging work constructing up a following, and if you are serving a neighborhood market and your purchasers are now not in the media or net business, it is likely a waste of time. Regular people do now not use Twitter.

On the different hand, you would possibly be in a position to use it to construct up a company presence if you are inclined to put in the effort. If not, at least you can furnish your opinions immediately to Donald Trump, however beware, your sturdy opinions can also be held in opposition to you.

## 4. Build Your Brand – Instagram

Instagram is the brand new toy for YouTubers, these in the media, and these with offbeat merchandise to promote their wares to teenage kids. If used successfully and imaginatively, it can create surges of viral visitors to your website.

## 5. Build Your Brand – Facebook

Everyone and their canine have a Facebook web page for their product, service, or their private brand. But pay attention of this, constructing up a following on Facebook is a lot much less beneficial applicable now than it used to be. Even if you have 5,000 humans who like your page, you can't actually talk with them until you pay Facebook; it is such a scam.

You ought to create a Facebook group, however make sure it is a non-public members-only team due to the fact if it is an open group, it will truely get spammed all day, each day.

## 6. Subscribe To Haro

Help a Reporter Out (Haro) is a definitely wonderful way to get some media insurance and construct your on line company and profile. It connects media journalists with enterprise experts. For example, in this article, I, as a media company, reached out to the Haro specialists to supply me their best suggestions to release opportunities. I acquired some extraordinary feedback, and it additionally permits me to construct greater contacts in the industry. Haro is free for contributing experts, and there is a month-to-month charge for media newshounds to use the service.

12 Ways To Create Career Opportunities
  1. Prove Your Value At Work
  John Showalter Founder: TightFistFinance

I had survived six rounds of layoffs at my company, and the seventh spherical was once coming. Management warned us, the seventh spherical used to be going to be brutal. People started to worry, and it grew to be obvious, no longer many human beings had ever deliberate that they may one day locate themselves jobless. I used to be organized with a fully-funded emergency fund and should stay off of my savings, however I would have desired no longer to dip into my savings.

Finally, the dreaded day came. One hour earlier than layoffs began, a high-level supervisor pulled me into an workplace and supplied me a new role inside the company, secure from layoffs. I took it barring hesitation. I would later locate out my direct administration line was once hostilities to shop me from the chaos. The following hours have been tough. A convention room used to be set up close to my cubicle, the place they exceeded out layoff notices. For the subsequent three hours, the room used to be a revolving door. We misplaced half of our team in a rely of hours.

So how did I role myself, so my administration fought to shop me?

Be a workhorse – Companies love it when you produce greater work than your peers, and it's now not challenging to do. Most personnel are caught on Facebook and now not working at work. Do your job, restrict distractions, and remain targeted on turning in your most important work tasks.

Be educated – Companies like it when you comprehend your job, and you do it well. No one wishes to pay a attorney to lookup the law; they would alternatively have the legal professional already be aware of the law. The greater you know, the quicker you can accomplish your main work tasks, which saves the employer money.

Make your boss's existence simpler – your boss is at once responsible for your pay increases. In my case, he tipped off top management that I may be on the layoff listing due to the fact he appreciated me and the work I carried out for him. I continually made his lifestyles less difficult and gave him severa victories. This was once his way of repaying me for making him seem to be exact all through the years.

Become useful – The greater competencies you acquire, the greater treasured you turn out to be to your company. If you are the solely man or woman at your organisation who is aware of how to use particular software, you are extra valuable. What occurs if you leave? The organisation is going to war and waste time ready for any person else to examine it.

Take on the challenging duties – No one desires to do difficult work at work, however pulling thru on a difficult undertaking makes you seem to be like a hero. Simply taking on the hardest duties at work makes your boss's existence easier, indicates anybody your a workhorse, and establishes you as any individual that is invaluable. Doing this one issue helps you stand out in so many ways!

2. Set Clear Career Goals

Ensuring you set clear profession desires that are in line with your values and philosophy is the key to making sure you continue the power and motivation to acquire these goals. Knowing your dreams will information you in the proper path when looking out for your opportunities.

How To Set Goals To Reach Opportunities:

Your purpose must be as unique as possible. Instead of "I favor to be precise at speakme to an audience," set the following profession goal: "I choose to make a profitable 10-15-minute presentation to an target market of at least 50 people.

Determine how you will measure success. What abilities will you develop? What work trip do you need? What certifications do you require?

Is the Goal is Achievable with the Current Plan? What will you want to commit in phrases of time and cash to make it happen?

Set the begin and cease date for attaining it. Setting time limits for every profession intention is imperative for your motivation and for reaching the preferred result.

3. Put Yourself Out There – Apply For Internal Jobs, Even If You Are The Unlikely Candidate

Yaniv Masjedi, Chief Marketing Officer at Nextiva

You want to put your self out there if you see an possibility really worth seizing. When I was once working to help my university education, I determined to take a jump of faith. The employer I was once working for was once opening up a advertising role whilst I was once working in sales. I requested the company's executives if they would reflect onconsideration on me, an undergraduate pupil with zero advertising background.

Now, they didn't have to be given me. But, I didn't have to ask and foyer for myself, either.

When you see an opportunity, you want to take the danger of stepping up to the plate. That's what I did – and 15 years later, I'm the proud CMO and Co-Founder of a 1,000+ group member corporation that spans more than one continents.

Of course, it took a lot of tough work and dedication in between – however I attribute a good deal of my success again to that preliminary choice to soar at an probability that excited me.

4. Make Sure Your Boss Knows You Want A Promotion

Now, this is now not the equal as asking your boss for a promotion. Informing your boss that you are involved in future profession development is the key here. You are no longer asking for a unique merchandising or position; you are letting them comprehend that you do desire to growth and develop inside this crew or company.

Do this earlier than any job openings show up and provide your self time to get in form for the step up and for your boss to see you in motion earlier than a new job opens up. Ask your boss what he thinks it takes to go up the ladder and what you can do to reap it. Simply letting your boss recognize that you would like to development will get you seen and open up attainable new opportunities.

5. Apply for New Jobs Externally

If you do now not sense you are getting the love, recognition, or possibilities you want in your modern company, the desire is simple, practice for a job externally. A find out about through the Guardian newspaper printed that surely altering jobs for a comparable function in some other enterprise yielded in 2018 an common 10% pay increase. Add the pay make bigger to the truth that you will be unlocking greater profession development opportunities, and you have a true decision.

6. Tips from an Attorney for Creating Work and Life Opportunities

Lance J. Robinson is a practising crook protection legal professional in New Orleans with over 22 years of experience.

As a crook protection lawyer and proprietor of my very own regulation company for over 20 years, I've discovered a lot about developing possibilities for myself. Here are a few of my preferred tips:

Have a clear set of goals. Knowing what you prefer to accomplish is the first step to discovering the proper possibilities to meet these goals. Always have 1-year, 5-year, and 10-year plans for your profession (or even your private life) to hold you on track.

Take calculated risks. Creating an chance for your self typically includes taking a risk. Be open to risk, however solely after you've executed your research. I had countless awesome jobs after regulation school, however I desired to take a danger and begin my very own firm. Once I had a diagram in place, I used to be in a higher role to create the possibilities I sought with my very own business.

Keep with the times. If I should supply my youthful self a piece of advice, I'd inform him to take science and the web greater seriously. Making positive you're conscious of developments and adjustments in the world will amplify your consciousness of new opportunities.

7. Speak to Strangers at Work

Even in the closed and tightly closed surroundings of the company office, most human beings do now not even recognize every other. Most people, in fact, solely understand their direct groups and a few different humans they have had conferences with. What would take place if you set a undertaking for your self to communicate to and introduce your self to one new individual at work each day?

By the give up of the year, you would be aware of over 250 new human beings backyard your team. That would make you the king of networking at the workplace and quite amplify your sphere of influence.

Imagine the possibilities that would unlock. Don't forget, though, after the interaction, write down their identify and describe them, so you have at least some threat of recalling them in the future.

8. Be At Your Best In Meetings & Events

One of my exceptional company possibilities got here after I delivered a stable presentation at a world company approach face-to-face meeting. I was once pretty junior in contrast to the series of Vice Presidents and Directors at the meeting. Three months later, I obtained a name from one of the attendees of that meeting, with whom I had constructed a properly rapport, and he supplied me a huge advertising and pay rise.

He instructed me without delay it used to be due to the fact he had met me in that assembly and preferred what I was once doing.

## 9. Build Momentum
Stacy Caprio. Founder: Growth Marketing

My great tip on developing work and existence possibilities is to create your personal small to as large as you favor success and momentum first. You'll locate as you begin having small wins, you'll robotically begin attracting extra possibilities in that area. You can even compound the variety of possibilities you entice for enterprise possibilities by means of going on podcasts, video & journal interviews, and for personal, you can put up small wins on your non-public social media bills to make bigger possibilities and consequences there.

## 10. Ask Your Boss How You Can Improve
If you design this properly in advance, you can acquire enter from your supervisor as to what they suppose it takes to get promoted to the job you want. A top probability is in your each year overall performance evaluation or any brain planning things to do that occur. Ultimately this is extraordinarily precious statistics as it will probable be your boss that awards you that promotion.

## 11. Get A Promotion Without Having To Ask
If you have to ask for a promotion, it's already too late; you

want to be a herbal choice.

There are 4 quintessential elements in getting promoted:

Deliver on your dreams consistently.
   Deliver your desires on time.
   Deliver your desires in the proper way with professionalism
& integrity.
   You are already a natural choice.
   [Related Article: Get Promoted At Work Without Asking]

12. Become A Leader
   You do now not want an legitimate invitation to be a leader;
you can take the lead on many things to do barring encroaching
on your manager's authority or developing resentment with
your teammates.

Offer to stand-in for your boss throughout vacations.
   Organize work occasions and get-togethers
   Volunteer to characterize your crew to different groups and
organizations
   Offer to lead group meetings.
   Be a idea chief by way of planning in advance and discovering
unique subjects of pastime to the group or team objectives.
   These movements will get you observed and unencumber
future opportunities.

11 Ways to Create Business Opportunities
   1. Purchase An Existing Business
   Nick Haschka, Partner Cub Investments. Nick is an skilled
innovation leader, increase strategist, and entrepreneur with

know-how in sustainable business, foremost avenue investing, and finance.

I bought a profitable 40+-year-old small enterprise from a retiring proprietor the use of a small commercial enterprise loan. It's created a pleasant job, and I develop fairness in the enterprise as it grows and as the mortgage receives paid back. There are so many magnificent small companies out there that want new proprietors due to the fact any person wishes to retire. If you recognize adequate about business, you can discover one, purchase it, and construct your profession round your lifestyles vs. constructing your existence round your career.

2. Be A Scrappy Entrepreneur

Paige Arnof-Fenn is the founder & CEO of international advertising and branding company Mavens & Moguls based totally in Cambridge, MA. She graduated from Stanford University and Harvard Business School.

I began a world branding and advertising association 18 years ago. I am a scrappy entrepreneur who tries to locate innovative methods to multi-task that accommodates work and exercise. When I labored at massive companies, they had gyms at the office or businesses who walked at lunch, however when you are an entrepreneur, you have to get innovative to locate balance. Instead of assembly up with your nearby colleagues at a espresso shop, over a meal, or chatting with them on the phone, meet them for a stroll so you can seize up whilst you are getting some exercising too. You'll sense gorgeous after the time will fly & it will be a exciting pastime to share.

It additionally works with customers; I have customers who play golf, so on occasion we meet at a using vary rather of the workplace to talk about things, specifically when you are making an attempt to suppose backyard the box. A alternate in venue is constantly nice, and you experience so a great deal higher when you are shifting and no longer trapped at the back of your desk.

The different suggestions I like to include are taking public transportation when possible, parking at the some distance stop of the lot, and strolling as nicely as taking the stairs as a substitute of the elevator; it provides up to a lot of more steps and motion if you do it each day. I suppose that respecting my time on the calendar and taking myself as critically as I take my most essential consumers is the least I can do due to the fact if I am now not at my

peak performance, I am no longer going to be beneficial to absolutely everyone else either.

Give your self permission to say no, whether or not it potential sound asleep in (no to an alarm clock), getting a massage, taking a walk, or simply turning off my smartphone and laptop (no, I will reply later on my personal schedule). I be aware of that my day has been profitable when I no longer solely assist my purchasers however additionally consist of easy acts of letting myself loosen up and revel in the moment; these are the very first-class presents I can supply myself that assist me continue to be balanced and productive.

3. Creating Opportunity from Remote Work
   Lydia Noyes.  Health, Wellness, and Lifestyle Journalist

HighYa.com

I began freelance writing on the aspect in early 2016 when I seen that my non-public weblog was once beginning to achieve traction, and human beings have been drawing near me with writing requests. After a few false starts offevolved on "content mill" web sites like Iwriter and Textbroker, I made a profile on Upwork and landed my first job ($15 for a 1,500-word article a few days later). This pay price was once abysmal, however I earned a five-star evaluation for the effort and quickly landed different jobs that had been notably extra profitable.

I finally branched out to touchdown semi-permanent writing jobs on job boards from web sites like Problogger, and after 4 months of freelancing, I determined to give up my day job and freelance full-time. In my first full yr of freelancing, I earned $50k pretax ($3,500-6,000 per month) and hit $65k in my 2d year. After freelancing for three years, I conventional a full-time far flung role with HighYa.com as a fitness and well-being reporter.

Freelance writing used to be some distance from what I deliberate to do as an adult, as I earned a bachelor's diploma in Environmental Studies. Still, I am always grateful for the possibilities that faraway work opened up for me. As an example, my husband and I bought a 33-acre farm property with my freelance writing earnings, which we are slowly turning into a dream interest farm. This potential we stay in a far flung location the place it would be challenging for me to discover usual employment, so freelancing is what makes our way of life financially sustainable.

103 Actionable Tips For Creating Opportunities Now Career & Promotion

## 4. Take Matters Into Your Own Hands

Shelley Mechette is an extraordinarily passionate Certified Life Purpose Coach and Women's Change Agent devoted to the empowerment of ladies via strategized private and expert development. ShellyMechette.com

### Host Your Own Events

It's no secret that we all choose to be profitable in life. Sometimes, possibilities simply do now not come the way we assume that they should. What do you do when you are over-looked for the merchandising or have reached a glass ceiling however be aware of that you are supposed for more? You step outdoor of your remedy sector and host/create your very own occasions based round your journey and expertise.

For example, if you have ride in the restaurant commercial enterprise and revel in cooking, host a networking tournament serving your personal entrees so that others can style your creations, inserting them in the function to want to turn out to be a future customer.

Suppose you are a teacher, host activities that will construct relationships between mum or dad and child, the use of your years of ride as a guide. Creating your very own activities to exhibit your Genius and knowledge will grant countless possibilities for you and future monetary rewards.

### Write About It

We all have a story. We all have skilled trials, disappointments, discouragement, and many different things. A notable way to create your very own probability is to write about what you have discovered in existence thru its hardships and your triumphs. We ALL want encouragement and to comprehend that any person else who has been the place we are…made it out on the different facet successfully.

When you write a book, you open up infinite doorways to success. You open your self to turning into the professional on what you have written about, speakme opportunities, workshop facilitating, and more! There is continually anybody in need. Someone is constantly ready for the equipment wished to aid them in winning. Your story simply may also be the very possibility to grant what you BOTH are searching for.

Get on the Phone & Offer Services

We are residing in a large science world. We talk via email, text, and social media. Sometimes, however, it's top to go again to the major way of communication…PHONE CALLS.

You can create high-quality possibilities for your self by way of getting on the phone, contacting decision-makers of companies, and supplying your offerings to them for free. If you recognize quite a number software program programs, provide to install/upgrade theirs for free, then ask them to provide you three commercial enterprise referrals so that you are in a position to do the equal for them.

This will set up your business/expertise, construct your contacts, and sooner or later function you to reap financially. By presenting your services, you will be in a position to create a monetary legacy for your household and emerge as the CEO of your life and time!

## 5. Work Remotely – Make Time For Side Hustles

Not all people has the chance to make use of bendy working or far off working. Many human beings are compelled to travel to an workplace each and every day. If you already work from home, then you truely have a lot extra flexibility to format your day and work.  If you have some quiet time throughout the working day, you can work on yourself, your future career, or plant the seeds of a new commercial enterprise (see Start a Sidehustle below).

If you desire to strive to affect your administration or HR group to introduce bendy working, then take a appear at our article "Benefits of Remote Working for Employers."

## 6. Start a Side Hustle

Side Hustles are the subsequent massive issue that already happened. A facet hustle is a small enterprise or aspect job that you begin while working in your cutting-edge job. If you have the flexibility and manipulate to free up time in your day, you can begin a aspect enterprise to convey you extra income. If it runs successfully, your aspect hustle can also develop into a fully-fledged enterprise that can preserve you financially and possibly even set you financially free.

Listen to my preferred Podcasts on aspect hustling referred to as The Side Hustle Show with Nick Loper; each and every episode will free up new thoughts and doable possibilities in your mind.

Here are some examples of the commercial enterprise thoughts featured on this show.

Piano Lessons
    Growing microgreens
    Strength training
    Baking sourdough bread
    Hiring digital assistants
    Picking up trash
    Starting after college programs
    7. Solve A Problem That You Face
    Esha Herbert-Davis is an tournament planner with over 20 years of experience. She plans special and life-changing Caribbean experiences for female who don't have the time or strength to sketch their personal magnificent vacations.

My husband and I identified the probability when we had been each speakme about our first time going to Trinidad Carnival. We realized that we each skilled frustration when attempting to coordinate our journeys there. Online assets and records about what occasions to go to, how to get tickets, and the place to remain had been extraordinarily limited.

Then we thought, there are possibly different human beings out there who sense the identical frustration. Are there team programs that do all of the coordination for human beings who prefer to ride this incredible festival? After being unable to locate any all-inclusive options, Ultimate Trinidad Carnival used to be born. We had been the first all-inclusive Trinidad Carnival supplying in the market returned in 2011. Seizing this probability potential we get to work in a commercial enterprise and share a subculture that we stay and work with extraordinary consumers from round the world!

8. Turn a Trend Into A Business or Start a Trend
  Lacey Mayer, Van existence Influencer & Founder SDCampervans.com

I used to be depressing working for what I notion was once my dream job. I put in years of training solely to locate myself enslaved to a system. This device is failing our society, however I located a neighborhood that supplied a extraordinary outlook on life. We moved into a van, acquired far flung jobs, and started out traveling. We go to the beach, go biking, and do different matters we love intermittent with working remotely each single day. We will by no means lock ourselves into 4 partitions and work ourselves to the core, solely to earn a small paycheck for our offerings ever again. The NEW RICH capacity you have TIME to spend on yourself, your family, your friends, your community, and your passions, no longer money to spend on gadgets you assume make you happy. We ARE happy.

With our companies, we make proudly owning a domestic and doing what you love to do at the identical time handy to the public. We do this through constructing dream homes, simply on wheels! People are asking themselves extra and extra every day, "What is this 9:00-5:00 surely doing for me if I'm miserable?" This way, though, is the new way to live, work, and journey AT THE SAME TIME.

SD Campervans builds out tiny houses entire with our female touches (we are a majority women-owned and operated company) such as backsplashes, builder oak countertops, recessed lighting, and shiplap ceilings. These properties are on wheels and geared up to go anyplace your subsequent journey takes you.

9. Find A Business Partner In An Existing Business

Another way to create a enterprise chance is to purchase your way into an present enterprise as a co-founder or partner. This has the gain of you hitting the floor jogging in an current commercial enterprise with any one who already has experience. Of course, you would want to be well matched with the character and have capabilities that are complementary to theirs. You should begin your search at Startups.com

10, Do What No-one Else Is Doing

Rishit Shah is CEO and Editor at TallySchool.

While doing my CA course, I realized an accounting software program referred to as Tally. At that time, I had some issues whilst working in Tally. So, I seemed up the net to clear up my problem. To my surprise, there have been very few web sites which have been providing good

solutions to the trouble I had.

And, therefore, I noticed an possibility there. I created my very own internet site referred to as TallySchool, the place I started out instructing Tally.

In round six months, it took off and used to be actually nicely obtained by way of the people. Today, it is one of the pinnacle web sites the place human beings come to study Tally.

11. Turn Your Passion Into Your Work

Sahara Rose De Vore empowers vacationers to take manage and sketch their dream life-style so they can have the transformative and impactful journey experiences that they crave. The Travel Coach Network

When I graduated from University in 2010, I had no clue what my best profession direction was once no matter having a bachelor's diploma in tourism. I knew about the job choices that exist, and I knew about the developing digital nomad jobs, however none of that truly resonated with me. I've in no way been anyone who observed the norm either.

I didn't desire to go the regular route in lifestyles from college, mountain climbing the company ladder, getting married, shopping for a house, and having a family. Do I favor some of those? Absolutely but, I desire them on my personal terms. The summer time after graduating from college, I packed my bag for the first time, and off I went to tour the world. I used to be capable to shop ample money after making mild changes in how I budgeted and managed my money. I was once hoping that journey would assist me analyze who I was, what I desired out of life, and what my cause is.

I knew I desired extra out of life, and I desired a profession that aligned my passions and motive with how I earned a living. I desired to create my very own lifestyle, the place I didn't sense constrained or constrained on time or money. I have constantly displayed this notion through working quite a number atypical jobs that I loved doing, which taught me new skills, and that had been bendy with appropriate pay, which is how I afforded to tour the world. Since 2010, I have traveled to over eighty nations by way of the age of 30 on my own.

Since I knew the characteristics that I desired in a career, and I knew how handy it used to be to have the profession you dream of due to the fact the web and science allow it, I used to be decided to discover what I was once supposed to do. I allowed time and my tour experiences to encourage my profession desire as a tour teach and beginning my very own on line business. I have usually created possibilities for myself through making an attempt new things, getting to know about whatever and the whole thing I could, assembly and speakme with new people, and difficult myself to study what I used to be suitable at, what I loved doing, and what my weaknesses were.

I took the bounce and invested in myself no longer solely via journeying however additionally in mentors who I admired in the teaching and commercial enterprise industries. I had to analyze how to ask for help, and when I ultimately did, it modified the complete trajectory of my profession path. I started out analyzing as a whole lot as I ought to about the tour industry, about being a coach, about the voids and issues that existed in the tourism and hospitality industries. I meshed that records with the whole lot that I knew, experienced, and discovered whilst traveling. I used my time travelling as an probability to do my very own market lookup and have hundreds of conversations with human beings all over the world about tour trends, why human beings traveled, journey jobs, and lots more. This is what all lead me to format my dream profession that is thriving today.

The advantages that I have obtained from growing these possibilities for myself consist of being in a position to assist others format their very own dream lifestyle, supporting vacationers align their ardour for tour with their purpose, discovering my very own life-long cause as a journey coach, being capable to develop my enterprise to its very best practicable that fits my imaginative and prescient for it, being financial, time, and spiritually free, and having typical happiness.

Some recommendations that I would have on developing work and existence possibilities are:

Use your resources. Learn as plenty as you can about some thing you prefer online, in books, and from different people. The world is crammed with so a good deal reachable free information; it's up to you to use it.

Build true connections with people. Learn from all of us and everyone. Everyone has some thing to teach.

Ask for help. Find anybody who is doing or has achieved some thing that you choose and ask for help, guidance, or mentorship.

Invest in yourself. This can be enriching your lifestyles with travel, investing in a teach or mentor, or investing time to study and begin a business.

Follow your personal path. It doesn't remember what society, friends, or household count on or think. Live your lifestyles for your self and diagram your best lifestyle.

Try new things. The greater matters you attempt (jobs, hobbies, etc.), the greater you will analyze about what you like, don't like, and favor out of lifestyles and career.

Challenge your self and make mistakes. Making mistakes is key to accelerating your route to discovering your reason and imaginative and prescient in lifestyles or business.

6 Ways to Create Opportunities Through Relationships
   1. Meet With New People
   Martin Luenendonk is a data-driven enterprise innovator and the Co-Founder & CEO of Cleverism, which is an on line job portal packed with heaps of special jobs in each and every field.

Look for humans and co-workers who are on the equal path. These humans can inspire and encourage you to do splendid matters in life. Spend some time and begin networking with like-minded humans who share the area with you. Socializing does no longer in reality suggest greeting every different on social media networks or speak through emails.

Personal interplay is extraordinarily vital if you virtually desire to analyze something. Try to be part of the neighborhood meet-up groups, enterprise conferences, or occasions associated to your field. This way, you extend the probabilities of assembly new human beings who can create new opportunities for you and assist you attain your goal.

For example, if you are an entrepreneur searching for an investor, there are possibilities that with positive conversation and by using pitching a excellent enterprise idea, you may additionally discover a accurate investor. So, assembly new humans constantly convey gorgeous opportunities.

103 Actionable Tips For Creating Opportunities Now Career & Promotion

2. Online Mastermind Groups – Unlock Great Possibilities
   David Leonhardt is President of THGM Writers, serving small agencies and individuals.

The very excellent chance generator for me has been mastermind communities. These are on line chat organizations committed to a positive subject of interest. You can locate these on LinkedIn and Facebook, though my desired gatherings are in Skype chat rooms.

In my case, I am in a range of chats unique to expert writing, blogging, and marketing. People put up questions; they seem to be for collaborators, they provide opportunities, and they share their work sometimes.

The advantages of participating in these chat rooms are severa and on-going.  I have had the possibility to subcontract on higher contracts. I have had free offerings for my business. I have determined possibilities to promote my commercial enterprise for free or for a fee, as these frequently get announced. I have had the threat to visitor publish on the blogs of different participants. I have located subcontractors to assist me entire projects. And I've gotten a lot of recommendation when I've been caught or unsure about something.

Networking usually opens the doorways to opportunities.  I used to belong to a BNI (Business Networking International) group, which is offline networking. But on-line mastermind communities are even extra beneficial for opening up opportunities, particularly for corporations no longer constrained with the aid of geography.

3. Create Your Own Mastermind Group

There is no higher way to generate ideas, opportunities, searching for help, and provide assist to others than thru a mastermind group. If you don't discover a mastermind crew to provider your desires in your vicinity, why now not create your own. Reach out to people you appreciate and ask them if they are interested.  It is a incredible honor to be requested to be part of a mastermind group, and most entrepreneurs recognize the benefits

Use Industry Societies or Associations To Generate Leads & Opportunities

Most great enterprise or expert associations will have a ordinary e-newsletter or periodical. But what they additionally do is run normal functions, get-togethers, or dinners. Attending these meetups and social features will provide you get entry to to a wealth of know-how and new connections. Don't neglect to convey your enterprise cards.

4. Unleash the Power of Local Meetups

Meetup.com is the powerhouse at the back of the majority of nearby meetup communities.  It offers the framework for organizing, gathering participants, and speaking with the attendees. If you have no longer tried it, head on over to the website. I am positive there will already be a nearby meetup in your region of interest.

5. Join Online Communities

If you can't attend in person, the different choice is to be part of an on line neighborhood of like-minded people. The net is full of them, and certainly there are over one hundred communities with over a million participants. Indeed there may additionally be massive on-line communities, however how beneficial are they to enhance your network? Definitely no longer as fine as neighborhood meetups or mastermind groups. However, the large benefit of on-line communities would possibly no longer be to improve significant members of the family however extra to apprehend future opportunities. As referred to previously, attempt this.

Locate the applicable on-line communities that have message boards and contribute. It will provide you the probability to analyze from others, and even extra importantly, you can see what questions humans ask and what wants and lack of expertise they have. You can even study from these who bitch online, as humans who whinge normally are sad with the provider or product; you can then assume about the multiplied offerings and merchandise that would meet their needs.

6. Use Your Family Network

Although frowned upon via these who do now not have a sturdy household network, nepotism is nonetheless rife. Indeed the Washington Post wrote a scathing article into the Trump family's nepotism. So robust favoritism of household individuals with whole brush aside for capacity is typically now not a correct idea, however that does now not suggest your household participants can't liberate the door to possibility for you, ask round there ought to be a acquainted assisting hand.

6 Ways Speaking Creates Opportunities

1. Join Toastmasters & Open Doors

Being in a position to without a doubt and intelligibly get your factor throughout is quintessential in today's enterprise world. Your phrases need to additionally imply something. But it is now not what you say; it is additionally how you say it.

All of us, from the CEO to the man or woman contributor, can enhance our speakme skills. If you severely desire to develop your self assurance and engagement, the single exceptional way to do it is through becoming a member of the not-for-profit organization, Toastmasters. I used to be a member myself for two years.

Not solely will your public talking enhance dramatically, however you will additionally community and in reality get to be aware of some extraordinarily fascinating people. I have met CEOs, commercial enterprise owners, actresses, and human beings with implausible charisma. When you are a assured speaker, you can cross on to the subsequent tip.

2. Paid Speaking Engagements Across The Globe
   Galit Ventura Rozen is an award-winning expert speaker, entrepreneur, commercial enterprise overall performance expert, and industrial actual property broker.

By networking without a doubt and in-person, I have created relationships and am recognised as an specialist in my discipline of business, mindset, and entrepreneurship.

Those that I meet are no longer usually without delay the ones that are fascinated in hiring me; many times, they are telling others in their community about me, and then every other enterprise will attain out. Referrals are the fantastic way to develop your business. This is performed by way of connecting with others and asking how you can advantage and assist their business, and it has grew to become round tenfold to advantage my commercial enterprise as well.

## 3. Speak At Industry Events & Seminars

Becoming a visitor speaker or keynote speaker at any tournament will release a new world of opportunity. I have been invited to communicate at many company occasions over the years, and they truly get you recognized. People admire these that can get up and speak, and if you are good, they would possibly even hear your message. Even being requested to communicate is an acknowledgment of your influence.

## 4. Ask A Question – Get Noticed

Whether you are in a assembly at work or a public gathering, or a seminar, if there is an probability to communicate up and be heard, take it, even if it is clearly asking a question. Even if it makes you experience uncomfortable, you need to get into the addiction of interacting with audio system and audiences.

## 5. Go On Podcasts or Radio

OK, so now you have the experience, you have the expertise, and you have your private brand. But you favor to attain a wider target audience to free up even extra opportunities. You should generate pastime by means of performing on Podcasts or even radio shows. But how do you get these gigs? Try Help a Reporter Out.

4 Ways To Create Friendship Opportunities

1. Online Dating Is Out – Use Meetup

A proper buddy of minds has been single for many years, and even although he has tried all the primary on line relationship agencies, he has been unsuccessful in attracting any achievable partners. It can also be due to the fact he has a "face for radio," and notwithstanding being successful, charismatic, and an all-round terrific guy, when you are genuinely judged by using a image of your face, it is a shallow and negative experience.

He then had the brainwave to attend occasions via meetup.com, and though Meetup.com, no longer a courting site, he joined a team referred to as "The Cocktail Crawl," which was once a crew of 20 girls that met up and crawled the bars consuming cocktails. He used to be the solely man in the group, and he stated he had a high-quality time.

2. Join A Recreation or Sports Club

If you revel in bowling, hiking, climbing, tennis, golf, or any form of bodily activity, there will be a neighborhood membership for you. Although the human beings in the membership may no longer be aligned with an enterprise or your outlook, you will nonetheless have a giant probability to make some significant friendships. And barring buddies and family, what do we have? Nothing.

3. Become President Of A Sports Club

If you are in a membership lengthy enough, you may have the chance to run for president of the membership or even one of the senior roles like treasurer. This will provide you the possibility to get to recognize all the participants and even welcome aboard new members, substantially broadening your circle of acquaintances.

## 4. Travel To Meet Interesting People

For me, backpacking is the first-rate way to meet fascinating people, and the extra uncommon the location, the better. But do now not fall into the lure of hiring a auto and using everywhere. The locations you meet humans are on buses, trains, in stations, and on the trekking trails. The excellent element is that the humans you have a tendency to meet when visiting the world have a tendency to be broadminded, liberal, adventurous, and fun. Now these are my variety of friends.

## 4 Ways to Create Opportunities from Everday Situations

### 1. Introduce Yourself At The Watercooler

Try this, the subsequent time you drop by way of the water-cooler for a fresh drink, introduce your self to the subsequent individual that comes along. Do this frequently enough, and you will understand absolutely everyone in the company, now that is a true network.

### 2. Join Company Sports Clubs

A exquisite vicinity to meet new humans is at company sports activities golf equipment and carrying events. Any business enterprise of widespread measurement will generally have a jogging club, tennis club, or at least a organization gym. Attend these clubs, and over time you will get to be aware of all and sundry there. And if your employer is web hosting charity events, take part.

### 3. Hang With The Smokers or The Drinkers

How if you experience smoking and drinking, then you will

likely be aware of this secret. Hanging with the people who smoke on their smoke smash is actually one of the gorgeous methods to meet people. Smokers are a marginalized minority, and what do with be aware of about minorities, they stick together, and they talk.

Now drinkers love a appropriate chat and a laugh; if you go out for a celebration night time with a bunch of drinkers, you are assured to have the begin of some accurate chum relationships.

103 Actionable Tips For Creating Opportunities Now Career & Promotion

4. Works Functions Are The Best Networking Opportunities.
   You have to constantly attend work functions, such as parties, celebrations, and income kick-offs. If there is a leaving celebration for someone, you need to be there. There is no higher way to meet human beings and deepen relationships than over drinks with colleagues. Alcohol lowers inhibitions, and you will locate you can talk about matters with your boss or new associates that you should in no way broach in the office.

4 Ways Charity Creates Opportunities
   1. Creating Opportunities for Others
   Believe it or not, growing possibilities for others is a jointly really helpful transaction. For example, it is regularly said…

"THE SIGN OF A GOOD LEADER IS THEY CREATE OTHER GOOD LEADERS"

This is, in fact, very true. For example, if you, as a manager, instruct and mentor your group contributors and promote them in the organization, they will in no way overlook that. If you are a accurate chief with a splendid relationship with them, you are, in fact, constructing a sturdy circle of influence; these humans will talk noticeably of you, aid you and be there for you.

People desire the equal matters as you, respect, dignity and to be valued; supply them what they need, and you will be paid again in full.

## 2. Help Others: Give Your Time To People In Need

In many of the examples so far, we have mentioned how to create possibilities for you in your business, career, and friendships. But what about others that want opportunities? Will you assist them? After the Syrian refugee crisis, our city acquired about 30 refugees from Africa. I determined it was once remarkable how a section of the town's neighborhood volunteered their assist and shaped a refugee committee. My spouse and I helped also. We made pals with some and helped them as a good deal as we could. My spouse was once even named as godmother to one of their children. Opportunities come in many shapes and sizes; this was once the chance to assist others and do some thing altruistic. Try it.

## 3. Sponsor A Local Charity Event

There are charity occasions taking place all the time; get involved, do a charity run; if you can't run, attempt contributing in every other way, sponsor the event. Sponsoring is a first-rate way of supporting due to the fact you will donate cash to the tournament and, in exchange, get a point out on a leaflet or poster for the event. You can then write it off towards the advertising budget; it is a win-win.

## 4. Give Your Time To Charity

Five years ago, my spouse had the probability to tour to El Salvador with a charity known as Giftasmile, which helps adolescents in poverty in Telangana. She used to be there for 4 weeks to instruct the youth and assist paint and restore the jungle village. Now that is giving time to charity. But what did she achieve from this? She met any other lady who is now one of her high-quality friends, she had some magnificent tales and experiences, and she had a precise feeling in her heart; what greater motivation do you want to assist others.

# About the Author

Avancha Krishna Mohan is the author of 61 books and counting. He is best known for his works like AAn AAlphaa, Search Engine Optimization Secrettss Unveiled, Veni Vidi Vici: How to Win and Achieve All That You Want from Life!, Pitamaha Bheeshma! The Commander for Your Company! , The Perfect Crime!!!  Aandologix:  Kickstart your startup with the best strategy! He is also carrying more than 18+ years of experience in Digital Marketing and marketing as a whole.

**You can connect with me on:**

- https://vancriskhom.com
- https://twitter.com/avanchak
- https://www.facebook.com/avanchakm
- https://g.co/kgs/GWGrSK